GRIBBLE, Le
Famous Detective Feats

10 JAN 1978	17. OCT. 1978	15. SEP. 1979
18 FEB 1978	18. DEC. 1978	13. OCT. 1979
23 FEB 1978	−9. JAN. 1979	22. NOV. 1979
28 FEB 1978	−7. FEB. 1979	
30. MAR. 1978		
−8. APR. 1978		
29. APR. 1978		
15. JUN 1978	23 FEB 1979	17 MAR 2003
−6. JUL. 1978	23 MAR. 1979	
−5. AUG. 1978	23 APR 1979	
30.	22. MAY 1979	
30. AUG. 1978	23. JUN. 1979	
30.	20. JUL 1979	
14. NOV. 1978	20. AUG. 1979	

This book must be returned on or before the last date entered above otherwise a fine will be charged.

Books will be renewed, on application, unless they are required by other readers.

CL 15

FAMOUS DETECTIVE FEATS

Famous Detective Feats

LEONARD GRIBBLE

ARTHUR BARKER LIMITED
5 *Winsley Street London W1*

ISBN 0 213 00383 X

Printed in Great Britain by
Bristol Typesetting Co. Ltd, Barton Manor, Bristol

In memory of Scotland Yard's two Charlie Artfuls,
both of whom were my friends

CONTENTS

AUTHOR'S PREFACE

In this collection of a dozen stories of crime and of detective ingenuity, patience, and perseverance in different countries, and all of them except one at various periods of the present century, I have included some deservedly well-known cases with others not at all well known but which stand good comparison in their present company.

The same may be said of the detectives featured. Some are internationally renowned, while others could be met for the first time inside the covers of this book.

Each story, in its different way, illustrates the continuing conflict between those who have scant regard for the law and others whose careers have been devoted to the maintenance of the law and the protection of the general public. As such, they are all stories with a message for the seventies, an age when violence and lawlessness have attained peaks – or depths if one prefers – that could not have been imagined by some of these former stalwarts in the service of the ordinary man and woman menaced by criminals in the underworld of yesterday and the day before.

The themes vary as much as the settings, yet in each case the challenge is clear and is met in a way that commands the reader's admiration, for these are all, firstly and lastly, human stories – about people whose actions were dictated by their very human failings and frailties, and other people who learned how to read those actions aright as anti-social emotional explosions.

One story is set in the Yukon, where a craving for gold tossed men of vastly different upbringing and natures into an amazing melting-pot of humanity. Another has for its setting a Welsh valley where siblings vanished unaccountably. A car accident in

New York contrasts strongly with the capture in London of a man who at night wore a black mask.

Murder is enacted on a crowded French train hastening to the Riviera in the holiday season and in a deserted garage in the south of England, in a quiet corner of Amsterdam and in a busy German city.

There is the story of a clever American killer who had a passion for a fragile flower, of another who was an illiterate, of a seafaring man in Paris who liked cats and so died, and of a killer who slew in a royal household and yet was arrested because of something that had happened months before in a place hundreds of miles distant.

Such stories are in every way as original and as gripping as crime fiction and yet for the discerning reader they have an additional appeal no fiction can offer – the events described and the dramas enacted really happened.

They match events and dramas that are taking place all over the civilized world today.

1 THE CLUE OF
THE KEY RING

For several years after the historic Trail of '98 had flooded Canada's Yukon and Klondike regions with gold seekers desperate for sight of the yellow metal, the human inflow continued. Mostly these fortune hunters came from Skagway, in Alaska, after they had stepped ashore from steamers that had brought them north from seaports all along the Pacific seaboard of North America. From Skagway they had trudged hopefully over the notorious Chilcoot Pass towards White Horse and the creeks and river tributaries that were supposed to conceal untold riches in raw gold awaiting to be dredged from their mud and slime.

Among the gold seekers could be numbered many hard-grained criminals, from the United States, from Canada, even from Europe and Australia. These were the men whose violence and greed brought tragedy and death to the Frozen North. Against them the few stalwarts of the North-West Mounted Police stationed in the region fought a continuous battle. The victories they won tamed a wild land and created a legend that is often related seventy years later.

One of the most fascinating cases successfully closed by the Mounties at this time was the one that became known in their records as the Boat 3744 Murder. It was solved in circumstances that would test many a modern detective equipped with resources vastly superior to those aiding the Mounties in the Yukon in the first years of the present century.

The case opened within a few days of a new Assistant-Commissioner of the North-West Mounted Police arriving in Dawson, the Yukon's capital. This was the formidable Z. T. Wood, known as ' Zach ' to every Mountie in Canada's North-West. He had made police history by refusing to be intimidated by the notorious Soapy Smith in the gold rush days of 1898, when Soapy and his ruffians controlled Skagway. Single-handed Zach Wood had confronted the Soapy Smith gang and escorted a fortune in Yukon gold to a waiting steamer.

The new Assistant-Commissioner arrived to take up his fresh post in Dawson on 1 July 1902, and almost his first order was sent to the organization known as the River Watch, instructing them to make increased efforts to check the movements of all small craft using the river system in the Yukon. There was an export tax levied on gold leaving the country. Some of the more wily prospectors who had been successful tried to evade paying the tax by taking to boats instead of tramping overland. The observers of the River Watch had the task of preventing this. They camped out along the rivers at unlikely places, and the number of successful tax evaders became progressively fewer. Wood decided to tighten the net until evasion was well-nigh impossible.

However, the River Watch counted among its human hauls quite a few adventurers who had lost all interest in gold and the easy life it could purchase in cities thousands of miles distant from the Yukon. The River Watch kept a sharp lookout for bodies floating in the rivers and creeks and backwaters. Not a few were found, a large number of whom had died violently.

Constable Cudlip worked with the River Watch detachment based on Indian River. He was a typical Mountie of the kind who tamed the Yukon. A few months before Zach Wood became Assistant-Commissioner some trigger-happy ruffians had held up the Dominion Saloon in Dawson. One of them was a desperado named Bill Brophy. He was caught in a shack by Cudlip and two other constables dressed as Yukon toughs. In the fight to get their man Brophy was accidentally wounded by a shot from another Mountie. His wound didn't prevent Brophy putting up a despertae fight to avoid being jailed.

It was this same Constable Cudlip whose sharp eyes saw a suspicious object floating in the Indian River. As he had no ready means of reaching it he set off for Dawson, where he reported that the object looked like a man's body. Zach Wood questioned the constable personally, and was assured this was not a case of a man's imagination playing him tricks. He sent for Inspector D. M. Howard.

'Constable Cudlip has reported a floating object that could be a body,' Wood told the inspector. 'I suggest you and Corporal Piper take a canoe and bring it in. You could go up in the evening steamer.'

The next morning they were in the Indian River area, where the canoe was launched and Wood's emissaries started to hunt for the body Cudlip had seen. They found it eventually on the muddy bank of a backwater, where it was left when the river level dropped. The date was 15 July, and it was mid-summer on the Yukon, the trees in leaf, shrubs covered in foliage, and a warm sun shining from a cloudless sky. The sun's heat was causing the body to smell unpleasantly.

Inspector Howard left the canoe and splashed his way to the foul-smelling human remains. As he turned it over he felt vomit in his throat. The body was naked except for trousers and an overall trailing from one leg, below the knee. On the foot was a boot and a rubber overshoe.

The inspector moved an arm away from the mud-streaked body and saw what at first glance appeared to be a burn. He thought it was of a kind that might have been made by a bullet, but because of the advanced state of decomposition he could not be sure. After examining the dead man's trunk he moved the ghastly head and found a wound that oozed a stream of pinkish liquid. He and Piper studied the head wound and agreed that it could have been caused by a low branch overhanging the river against which the head caught as the body floated downstream.

But the inspector was not sure and decided there was one grim way to find out. He splashed to a willow growing on the bank and cut a slim branch from it. This he trimmed to make a probe which he inserted into the head wound. The stream of pinkish liquid gushed faster from the hole and then stopped, while the thin willow probe continued on through the head and finally protruded from another hole. Only a bullet could have torn such a channel clear through the head.

Whoever the man was, he had been murdered, which meant his identity had to be established without delay. The Mounties washed the trousers and overall, for they were stuck together with mud as firm as cement. As the mud was rinsed away they could feel some objects in one of the pockets. The objects proved to be keys held together on a key ring to which was attached a metal tab. There was lettering on the tab. When it had been cleaned they made out a name and address: Bouthilette was the name, and the address was 'East Broughton, Beauce Co, PQ.'

'If they were his keys, corporal,' said Howard to his companion, 'then he was a Canuck from Quebec.'

'That'll take time checking,' said Piper gloomily.

They rolled their grim find in some covering they had brought and dumped it in the canoe, then started the trip of forty miles back to Dawson, where the Assistant-Commissioner was waiting for their report. Wood ordered an immediate post-mortem, which resulted in the following conclusion being placed in the files:

'The man had been shot in the head twice with a heavy-calibre rifle and in the back with a revolver; the bullet coming out in front caused the burn.'

This report was offered to the coroner who held the inquest on the recovered body. His jury of Dawson citizens were addressed by Inspector Howard.

'Gentlemen,' he said, 'I must swear you to secrecy on a very important matter.'

This proved to be the bunch of keys and the tab on the key ring, which was offered as formal evidence of identity. The jury agreed to be bound to secrecy, and Howard was assured that there would be no idle talk in the town about the dead man's name or where he had come from. When the coroner had addressed the jury they returned their verdict.

'Murder against some person or persons unknown.'

Inspector Routledge, who was Wood's deputy in Dawson, sent a wire to White Horse, where a register was kept of all boats that were chartered for river work as well as the names of the men who left in them. Each river-boat was given a number, and into the record at White Horse went the date and place of arrival of each numbered boat that was chartered. In this way it was possible to follow where men hiring boats finally left them, so that the River Watch could keep a lookout for them when they moved on or made a return journey. This system of surveillance had been instigated by that veteran of the Yukon Superintendent

Sam Steele back in '98. Steele was another Mountie who became a legend in his own lifetime.

Thanks to Sam Steele's system of recording the movements of all river travellers passing through White Horse and beyond, Mountie Headquarters in Dawson did not have to wait more than twelve hours for the information it required. The records at the river control at White Horse showed that a man named Bouthilette had been a passenger in boat number 3744 when it left White Horse. That had been on 14 June, more than a month before. Accompanying Bouthilette were four other men, apparently all French-Canadians like the dead man. Their names were Beaudoin, Constantin, Ladoceur, and La Forest.

With this information in their possession the Royal North-West Mounted Police began some brilliant detective work. With Zach Wood in command of the investigation in his Dawson office, there was soon a sudden surge of activity in several directions at the same time.

Throughout the Yukon the Mounties started to make inquiries about the present whereabouts of the four men who had left White Horse in Boat 3744 with Bouthilette. At the same time a request was wired to Quebec for details and news of a man named Bouthilette who had lived at the address on the key ring's tab. Thousands of miles away from the Yukon plain-clothes men began making inquiries. They found where Bouthilette had lived in East Broughton and spoke to friends and relatives. Apparently the dead man had talked freely of his intention of going to the Yukon and trying his luck.

He had packed his things and left East Broughton on 4 June, bound for the Yukon. A letter had reached his home some time later announcing that he was writing from Vancouver, in British Columbia. The letter was dated 11 June, exactly a week after he had left home, and among the items of news was one which was important to the Mountie detectives. Bouthilette announced that he had made two new friends. Their names were Beaudoin and Constantin, and he was going to continue to Dawson in their company.

This information was wired to Dawson while the hunt for Bouthilette's companions continued. At the same time another search had been started. This was to find Boat 3744, which had apparently vanished without trace. Sergeant Smith in Dawson had no record of the boat reaching its understood destination, although a check had proved that boats preceding it had arrived safely, as had boats that had followed it. None of them had reported seeing Boat 3744 *en route*.

It was Constable Pat Egan who eventually discovered the missing boat, discarded in Klondike City. He was the constable whose gun accidentally wounded Brophy the hold-up man. Egan's find was taken down to Dawson, where it was examined thoroughly.

While this part of the case was taking definite shape, Superintendent Snyder in White Horse was filling in a dossier of facts collected by his own men. The two men from whom Boat 3744 had been hired were questioned. Their names were Rook and Cleveland, who explained that they had provided all the supplies the boat party of French-Canadians had required. The two partners in the boat business were also able to give the Mounted Police some reasonably accurate descriptions of the four wanted men. These were passed on to the various men trying to find the whereabouts of the missing four. A great deal of routine work was being done at this stage without very much to show for all the man-hours expended.

Then, on the last day of July, another body was found. Again it was a vigilant member of the River Watch who made the discovery. He was Constable Graham, whose patrol was maintained in the region of Ogilvie, which is about twenty miles from where Cudlip was stationed at Indian River. He reported to his superior, Inspector 'Buz' Jarvis, who collected the body and took it to Dawson.

When it was unwrapped at Mountie Headquarters there were exclamations of surprise. The head was missing. Who was this second dead man? That was another problem to be solved. Another inquest was held, and a second jury returned the same verdict as the first. They had been told that, according to the post-mortem report, the missing head had been blown off the dead man's shoulders.

The boat owners, Rook and Cleveland, were brought to Dawson from White Horse. They were taken to a makeshift mortuary and shown the headless corpse.

'That's Guy Beaudoin,' Cleveland said.

His partner agreed with him.

While they were in Dawson they were also questioned further about the boat party, but apparently they could not provide answers that had not already been given to Superintendent Snyder. They returned to White Horse and a fresh start was made to find the other three – Constantin, Ladoceur, and La Forest.

One of the Mounties working in plain clothes was Constable J. H. Burns, who spoke French fluently. He mingled with the crowds in various Dawson bars and saloons trying to pick up information without arousing suspicion. He was a remarkable detective in several ways, for he was prepared to take his own line while making inquiries. Moreover, he could think beyond the limit of known facts. It was this last quality that produced positive results. Burns realized that the men he was seeking might be known by other names.

Accordingly he began making discreet inquiries about French-Canadians who might have changed their names. In this way he came to hear of a pair who had gone around together and were known as Fournier and Labelle. They had disappeared sometime between early and mid-June. At least this was a time that could coincide with when Bouthilette and Beaudoin were murdered. Burns continued probing and buying drinks for men who might have information he wanted. He eventually found one or two persons who could tell him that Fournier and Labelle had in fact changed their names. They had called themselves in June Ladoceur and La Forest. Burns had crossed the missing men's trail.

His next success was the finding of a man named Charles B. Mack, who told the Mountie detective that he had fixed up to travel by boat to Dawson with Ladoceur and some friends of the other man. Ladoceur had kept telling him he was not ready whenever he made inquiries. Apparently the French-Canadian was awaiting the arrival of other friends, French-Canadians like himself, who would be journeying from Skagway.

'One day he came to me,' Mack told Burns, 'and asked me to be ready to travel the next day. This was short notice, but when I went to join him I was told the party had already left.'

Charles B. Mack was lucky to miss Boat 3744. His late arrival saved his life. However, having packed his gear and being ready to travel, he joined a later boat. On the way he saw the man he knew as Ladoceur in the boat he had missed. At that time Boat 3744 had five occupants.

Burns also spoke to a man who called himself Merriman. Like Mack, he too had agreed to join Ladoceur's party.

'Why didn't you go?' the Mountie detective asked him.

'I changed my mind.'

The result of Burns's undercover discoveries allowed the route of Boat 3744 to be traced with five occupants as far as Stewart River. There, quite suddenly, all further trace vanished. No one had news of it, no one had seen it. Stewart River was the limit of any inquiry that produced result.

Yet it was only a short fifteen miles from Stewart River to Ogilvie, where the headless body of the luckless Beaudoin had been first seen by Constable Graham. In the circumstances it was reasoned that the murders had been committed between those two places.

One other thing was fairly certain. The men wanted for murder had cleared out of the Yukon or effectively concealed themselves. The search was widened. It reached beyond the Yukon's boundary with Alaska.

A detective named Welsh arrived in Skagway and was shown back passenger lists of the steamship companies. He went back for a number of weeks before he found three names on his list. They were those of the trio who had sailed in company with each other from Vancouver – Bouthilette, Beaudoin, and Constantin. The three French-Canadians had arrived in Skagway aboard the steamship *Amur*. The inquiries made by Welsh suggested that he might find Seattle a port where he could be lucky in his quest for the other pair. He accordingly took a steamer to that American port.

As things turned out, he was on the trail of only one man, for it was the persistent Burns who eventually uncovered the wanted Fournier. By his persistence in making inquiries, even in unlikely places, and in following up clues of names that seemed to promise little hope of success, Burns found himself back in Dawson and trying to catch up with another man calling himself La Forest. Because Burns was not easily shaken, he found this other La Forest and received his reward when he first saw him face to face. The man was not another La Forest. It was the face of the man Rook and Cleveland had described as calling himself La Forest. But on Assistant-Commissioner Wood's latest list the man's name was Fournier.

Burns made sure he had really found his man's bolthole before he sent in his report. A conference was held at Mountie Head-quarters and it was decided not to arrest the man calling himself La Forest.

'He's to be put under a twenty-four-hour surveillance,' the Assistant-Commissioner ordered.

The tailing of La Forest night and day by some member of the Mounties in plain clothes began on 8 August. It continued until the 22nd, and not once was the man being watched allowed to suspect that he was being followed.

At the end of that two-week period Cleveland was asked to come up from White Horse. He was taken by Burns to get a good look at the man who had been tailed for a fortnight.

'That's La Forest,' he proclaimed. 'He was one of those who went with the other four in Boat 3744.'

La Forest was arrested. But in his own name of Fournier. He was the most astonished man in Dawson the day he heard him-self charged with murder. Before Cleveland returned to White Horse he was taken to see the boat that Pat Egan had found in Klondike City. Any number it had carried had been removed. But Cleveland knew his own property.

'When shall I get it back?' he asked.

'When the trial's over. It's wanted as material evidence,' he was told.

'The summer's getting past and we're losing money with that boat laid up,' he grumbled.

'Send the bill to Fournier,' he was advised sardonically. 'Boat 3744's still under hire to him.'

That was certainly true. Unfortunately for Cleveland and his partner Rook, Fournier was almost out of funds when he was arrested, and from the way things looked he wasn't going to be given an opportunity to reline his pockets.

Meanwhile Welsh was in Seattle, nearly fifteen hundred miles away, still trying to pick up the trail of Ladoceur, whose real name was by this time known to be Labelle. Indeed, it was in Seattle that Welsh discovered Fournier and Labelle had a police record in their own names. In that record they were filed as partners in violent crime. He wired Dawson. In reply he received another wire suggesting that Labelle might have made for Wadsworth in Nevada. This was an additional piece of helpful information picked up by the untiring Burns who, following Fournier's arrest, began making inquiries about the missing Labelle.

The other member of the trio that sailed from Vancouver, Constantin, was not sought as a wanted man. There was too much reason for supposing that, like the dead men whose bodies had been recovered, he had been murdered for what was in his pockets and luggage.

The Dawson end of the investigation was temporarily halted, awaiting the outcome of Welsh's long hunt for Fournier's known companion in crime. The relentless Welsh had made inquiries in six American States by the time he arrived in Wadsworth. He took care not to do anything to arouse the suspicion of the man wanted for murder after he had learned that the other was in hiding in the Nevada town. Labelle was not arrested until there was no chance of escape or of the French-Canadian's beating an extradition warrant.

But once in a police cell Labelle's determination to cheat the law crumbled. Within a few hours the man who had been worsted by brilliant detective work on the part of two members of a team working thousands of miles apart broke down.

'All right, I was Ladoceur,' he confessed to Welsh when the latter visited his cell. 'What do you want to know?'

'The truth will do,' Welsh said.

Labelle began talking like a man in a hurry to relieve his mind of something that has been a great mental burden. What he said was taken down by the patient detective. This prison statement was to provide most of the grim story that was later that year to shock two Canadian juries.

Labelle made one thing very clear beyond any doubt. The murders had been planned. They had not been the outcome of a sudden intention to kill for gain. The former partners in crime who had been known to the Seattle police had set up a scheme whereby they would collect any small party of new French-Canadian arrivals in the Yukon and offer them the chance to travel downriver from White Horse in the company of experienced guides who knew the country. Mack and Merriman had been possible extras to be included in the boat load.

As things turned out, the trio from Vancouver were anxious to lose no time starting from White Horse. Accordingly their brutal guides had not waited for Mack. After all, he might have changed his mind, like Merriman.

The plan was to take the newcomers to a lonely place along the river and there kill them, weight the bodies with stones, and dump them overboard. The victims' luggage would then be looted. What wasn't worth keeping would be burned and the telltale ashes scattered.

So Boat 3744 started from White Horse. The murderers spent that first night of 14 June camped with their victims. By that time they had agreed on a place which would be the scene of their crime. It was a small island about ten miles below Stewart River. The three chance travellers from Vancouver were shot in their sleep, their bodies robbed, and then tossed into the river.

When that was done the two killers added up the proceeds of their treachery and violence. They had acquired a total of a hundred and forty-five dollars and some few items of personal jewellery, none of it worth very much. To gain that three men had been murdered.

Terrible as this seems, there was more of a similar nature in Labelle's horrifying story. As though they were satisfied with these paltry gains from murder, the killers planned to repeat their villainy. While their victims' bodies remained concealed by the swollen summer flow of river water before two of them dragged free of their weight of stones, Fournier and Labelle approached another newcomer to the Yukon, Archie Gilbault, French-Canadian like themselves and their previous victims. They inveigled him into joining them on a similar trip. It was from Eagle City to Circle City, in Alaska. Somewhere along the river Gilbault was murdered for the cash he carried.

With Labelle's statement to guide them, two Mounties set out for that small island where the three companions from Vancouver had been shot as they slept. The place had no name, but Corporal Piper and Constable Woodill later referred to it as Murder Island. They found the place where the possessions of the murder victims had been burned and they returned to Dawson with sufficient pieces of tangible evidence to support Labelle's statement. The case was ready to be heard in court.

Labelle, who had been brought under escort from Nevada, stepped into the dock in Dawson's criminal court on 27 October to face a hard-eyed jury. It had taken the various members of the Mounted Police only forty-seven days to wrap up an investigation that had been conducted simultaneously at places two thousand miles apart. The only real clue provided at the start was Bouthilette's key ring.

Labelle's trial lasted four days. On the last day of October the jury, who had been shocked like everyone else in court by the grim recital of events, returned the expected verdict of ' Guilty ', and the judge sentenced the prisoner to death.

Four days later it was Fournier's turn to face a jury. The second trial was over in a single day, 4 November. Like his associate in violent crime, Fournier heard himself sentenced to die by hanging.

While the final processes of the law took their unhurrying course the old year gave way to a new one. It was a bitterly cold dawn when the sentences were carried out. The day was 20 January 1903.

The temperature in the prison yard where the gallows had been erected was fifty-two degrees below zero, an ironic touch to the conclusion of a grim story that had made listeners' blood run cold.

2 WHEN FEAR
ROAMED THE VALLEY

On an autumn day in 1953 Sir Ronald Howe, the Assistant-Commissioner at Scotland Yard in charge of the Criminal Investigation Department, sat in his first-floor office observing two men with interest. They provided a marked contrast to each other.

One was Detective Superintendent John Capstick, who had just been summoned to Howe's office. He was a thickset man with a square face and plenty of chin, who favoured bowler hats and Jaguar cars and smoked a pipe, and stared at the world around him with an inbuilt watchfulness that refused to let him be surprised by the unexpected. He was a detective with an impressive record of successes, a man known to be both respected and feared by the London underworld of that first decade following the Second World War, where he was either referred to by an unprintable name or by the grudging admiration to be found in the descriptive Charlie Artful.

The other was a Welshman, slimmer, who preferred soft felt hats and single-breasted coats. Like Capstick, he had started his adult life as a uniformed policeman, but administration rather than the detection of criminals had appealed to him, and he had made an outstanding career for himself.

These were the two men sizing each other up in Howe's office after the Assistant-Commissioner had introduced the Murder Squad detective to T. Hubert Lewis, the Chief Constable of Carmarthenshire.

When Capstick said, ' I'm glad to meet you, sir,' he meant it. The words were no formality. He had known of Hubert Lewis and admired him for a considerable time. Indeed, at a later date

23

Capstick said this of the Welshman he was meeting for the first time that day in Sir Ronald Howe's office: 'Starting his career as a uniformed constable with no influence to help him, he had made himself into one of the most efficient police chiefs in all Britain, and found time on the way to study law and become a barrister as well. That takes not only brains but real guts.'

Sir Ronald Howe told Capstick, 'Mr Lewis has been good enough to consult us about those curious disappearances.'

With those few words of brief explanation Capstick knew why he had been summoned to meet Carmarthenshire's Chief Constable. For more than two weeks the newspapers had been featuring a mystery in Hubert Lewis's county. A farmer named John Harries and his wife Phoebe had disappeared from their small farm of Derlwyn, at Llanginning, near St Clears. The village of Llanginning was about thirteen miles from the town of Carmarthen, which straddles the A40 road from London to Haverfordwest.

What had happened to John and Phoebe Harries?

That was the question neighbours and friends had been asking themselves and the police. The newspapers had asked the same question. The Carmarthen police had made a great many inquiries, talked to many people, covered many miles in their investigation, and found nothing pointing to a real answer. There was a great deal of suspicion, and most people around Llanginning seemed to have made up their minds to the worst. They believed John and Phoebe Harries were dead. It was a belief that posed a question of its own. What had become of the bodies?

The Chief Constable of Carmarthenshire was in London that day to enlist the help of Scotland Yard, and the job was Capstick's before he entered the Assistant-Commissioner's office to meet the Welsh visitor.

It was a strange and seemingly muddled story he was told then and later discussed with his own Murder Squad assistant, Detective Sergeant William Heddon, a man used to Capstick's ways and thought processes.

'This one won't be easy, Bill,' Capstick told Heddon, 'and our feet are going to ache before it's over.'

It was a true prophecy. Capstick had studied the detailed

report Hubert Lewis had brought to London and had found no short cut to the truth of the mystery that seemed to begin on Friday, 16 October. On that day John Harries and his wife, who was nine years younger, had gone to a funeral and returned home to prepare for a visit in the evening to Bryn Chapel, where a harvest thanksgiving service was to be held.

Harries was sixty-three, a man looking towards the closing years of a life spent in hillside fields and with cattle. He was also a man with a secret worry. His wife had been in poor health for some time past, and he felt the work of a farmer's wife on a modest valley farm wasn't giving her an opportunity to get better. Harries was a big man. He weighed sixteen stone. Like a great many big-framed men, he could be excessively jovial at times and at others lost in deep gloom. On that October Friday, after wearing his black tie and attending a funeral, he was somewhat oppressed by the thought of winter advancing to close another year.

When he arrived at Bryn Chapel for the special thanksgiving service he was a man with sadness shadowing his thoughts of harvest thankfulness.

He and his wife had walked to the chapel, which was not far by road from their farm. Normally they drove there in the family's Austin car, but over tea they had decided to walk after John had seen to the cows. After the service they stood outside the chapel talking to a neighbour who was also a farmer. His name was Morris and he suggested walking back to Derlwyn with the others. On the way they chatted about affairs in the valley and farm prices and the service they had just attended. Within a short while they were at the farm that was tucked away in a corner of the Taff Valley.

'You must come inside, Mr Morris,' said Phoebe Harries as their neighbour stood back to bid them goodbye.

The farmer hesitated and was persuaded by the woman's hospitable smile.

'Very well,' he said, 'but I can't stay long.'

They entered the farmhouse. The time by the clock in the sitting-room was shortly after half-past eight. Phoebe Harries filled a kettle to make a pot of tea. The kettle had still to come to the boil when a car pulled into the yard and a door slammed.

'Ron,' said John Harries.

A minute later his nephew Ronald Harries came into the room. He was smiling and nodded an affable good evening to Morris. He was twenty-five, rather short, with mobile features and crisp dark hair.

The visitor rose and glanced at the clock. The time was a quarter to nine.

'I'll be on my way now, John,' he said.

The farmer left, passing a Land-Rover in the yard, with no suspicion that he had said goodbye to John and Phoebe Harries for the last time.

The next development in the story Capstick outlined to Bill Heddon was the arrival at Derlwyn of a railway worker named Ronald James at half-past eight the next morning. He was surprised to receive no reply to his knock on the front door, and when he shouted there was still no response. The farmhouse seemed deserted, which was distinctly odd, for John Harries had cows to look after.

James walked round to the cowshed and opened the door. He was greeted by plaintive mooing from cows with bulging udders. It was not like John Harries to leave his cows unmilked. The railwayman left the cowshed and walked to the small garage. He found it empty. The family's black Austin was gone. It seemed odd, but then the answer might be very simple. The farmer and his wife might have been called away urgently at short notice.

Ronald James left Derlwyn. Two and a half hours later he was back, accompanied by his brother John. As they approached the Harries farm they saw two filled milk churns on a wooden stand by the roadside.

'They weren't there earlier,' Ronald James explained, surprised at seeing the churns.

The James brothers walked to the cowshed. They found that the cows had been milked and the shed swept out. The black Austin, however, was not in the garage.

'Looks like Ron came over and milked the cows,' said John James to his frowning brother.

Ronald Harries had certainly been in the vicinity that morning, for earlier he had called at the home of another Harries neighbour, Mrs Martha Powell, and explained that his uncle and aunt had left for London.

'For a holiday,' he said, 'and I'm looking after things till they return.'

He asked Mrs Powell if her son Brian could help him with the Harries cows. The woman readily agreed that her son, who was fifteen, could go to Derlwyn and help with the milking, but she was frankly surprised at the news of the couple going to London on the spur of the moment. To her mind, acting on impulse was not like them. On the Sunday Brian Powell went to Derlwyn and helped Ronald Harries.

The next morning Ronald Harries was alone at the farm when two friends of his uncle called. He told them, 'My uncle and aunt have gone to Pendine,' which was on the coast to the south-west of St Clears. Later another caller arrived, and this person was told that John and Phoebe Harries had left for London.

Capstick told Bill Heddon, 'After that it wasn't long before rumours started to circulate in the valley. You see, the missing pair weren't Ronald Harries' real uncle and aunt. Ronald's father, John Lloyd Harries, was a second cousin of the John Harries we've got to find.'

'If he's alive.'

'Or dead,' said Capstick grimly.

He explained to his sergeant that the young man who had been caught out in a lie was married and lived with his wife's family at Ashwell Farm, Pendine. He was the father of a child not a year old, and during the week he worked for his father at Cadno Farm, not far from Pendine and less than a dozen miles from Derlwyn.

However, although Ronald Harries came of a long line of Welsh farmers and was a good worker on a farm, he had no more cash than his father paid him in a weekly wage. It was not sufficient to allow him to indulge a weakness for driving anything fast on wheels along the wide stretch of Pendine's firm sands. Ronald's fondness for car racing was known to Phoebe Harries' brothers. When they called at Derlwyn and found Ronald in possession they listened to his story of the visit to London for a holiday but accepted it with a great deal of reserve.

'He's lying,' they decided when they left.

They went to the police. A constable called at Derlwyn. During his search, he went into the kitchen and opened the door of the oven. Inside, ready to be cooked, was a joint covered with greaseproof paper. It seemed distinctly odd that the couple should leave just before a week-end and forget the week-end joint. The Chief Constable of Carmarthenshire agreed with his constable. He had further inquiries started and then decided the mystery was a case for Scotland Yard to handle.

Ronald Harries, who told Capstick that his full name was Thomas Ronald Lewis Harries, seemed to the Yard detective to be a young man with a rather unstable personality. He appeared awed by this detective from London who was almost as broad-shouldered as his missing uncle. Or possibly Capstick's questions awed him. The Yard man had a great many to which he wanted answers.

Some of them received answers at variance with established facts. For instance, Ronald Harries assured Capstick that on that Friday night following the special harvest thanksgiving service at Bryn Chapel he had left his aunt and uncle at Derlwyn at a quarter-past nine. This meant he stayed for half an hour. But he claimed that when he left the farmer Morris was still seated in the sitting-room talking to John Harries. The nephew stated that he had said good-night and driven off in his Land-Rover. He had gone to Pendine because he had agreed to pick up his mother and father there. However, on the way, according to his story, he had stopped to help a farmer whose car had broken down.

'It was George Wilson,' he told Capstick. 'I gave him a tow to the gate of his farm.'

This was Middlepool Farm, where Ronald claimed to have left Wilson and continued to meet his parents. They had been waiting for him and he had driven them to Cadno Farm, where he stayed for supper.

'Then I went home to bed,' he said. 'I was very tired.'

Capstick wanted to know about the following morning. With Bill Heddon taking notes the now talkative young farmer explained that he had arrived at Derlwyn the next morning about ten forty.

'I found my aunt and uncle dressed up and was surprised,' he related.

Capstick wanted to know what he meant by dressed up, and he said they were dressed for going away and his uncle had come into the yard with a brown portmanteau, which he had put in the Austin's boot. While he was doing this Phoebe Harries was going round, in her nephew's phrase, 'locking up'.

'When she got into the car she gave me the keys,' Ronald Harries told Capstick. He had been asked to drive his uncle and aunt to Carmarthen, where they were taking a train to London. 'When we got there I parked the car, and as we had time in hand we went to the Willow Café.'

According to the nephew who was now remembering details with surprising clarity, they had entered the café and taken seats not far from the cash desk by the entrance.

'My uncle bought three cups of tea and nine cakes.'

It seemed satisfactory as far as it went, but it didn't satisfy Capstick, who believed in the value of detail and was never impatient, characteristics that made him a success when senior officer of the former Ghost Squad.[1] He asked Ronald Harries to go over the route from the Willow Café. The young farmer seemed puzzled by the request, but explained how he had left the café and walked down the street, past the central market, and into King Street, where he had stopped.

'My aunt wanted to go to a shop,' he said.

'Did you go with her?' he was asked.

He shook his head. 'No, I stayed in the car with my uncle.'

He went on to explain that he had parked near the door leading to the station's booking office. His uncle had got out and taken the brown portmanteau from the boot. Then he had gone into the booking hall and purchased the tickets, after which he had come back to where his nephew was waiting specially to say, 'Be a good boy, Ron, and do everything properly until we're back. We'll write to you, and don't lend anything to anyone.'

Capstick thought this a curious and even unlikely last request from an uncle going away suddenly on holiday and leaving his

---

[1] See 'Ghost Detectives' in the author's *Stories of Famous Detectives* (Arthur Barker Ltd).

nephew in charge of a farm where the cows had not been milked. There was no reference to when the couple might return and no address had been left with the nephew. For a normally careful and cautious man John Harries had behaved in a singularly inexplicable manner.

Later the Yard men questioned the waitress who had been serving in the Willow Café on the morning of Saturday, 17 October. She could neither remember Ronald Harries nor a party of three that ordered a cup of tea and three cakes each. After Ronald had told them which shop his aunt had visited in King Street the Yard men made another visit, but no one in the shop could recall serving Mrs Harries, nor could the booking clerk at Carmarthen Station remember serving any man fitting John Harries' description with tickets to London.

It was all nebulous and proved nothing except that Ronald Harries was a most unfortunate young man, particularly in the matter of the stubborn Mr R. W. Morris, who insisted to Capstick that he had left Derlwyn Farm a full half-hour before Ronald Harries said he did, and certainly before that young man himself.

However, it could be proved that Ronald Harries had been in Carmarthen on the Saturday morning he claimed, because some time between five past eleven and a quarter to twelve he had visited a solicitor named David Charles. Against this had to be balanced young Brian Powell's assertion that he had arrived at Derlwyn with Ronald Harries at half-past nine and remained there for two hours. Capstick wanted to know why it had taken an hour to get from Mrs Powell's to Derlwyn. He was told the young farmer and the boy had not gone direct to Derlwyn. Ronald Harries drove a black Austin to Cadno, where the pair were given some food, and then drove to Llanginning. On the way Ronald told Brian he had recently bought the car he was driving. He seemed to be enjoying himself at the wheel.

More disturbing than Brian Powell's story was the one told Capstick by a young trainee farmer named Desmond Baylis, who was working at Pendine.

Ronald told him, 'I've now taken over Derlwyn. My uncle has given me the five cows and all the farm implements.'

On the evening of the day Ronald made this claim the cows

and a calf were driven over to Cadno. The aunt and uncle had by then been missing for three days and the rumours had begun to circulate.

Another intriguing fact Capstick had to weigh was Ronald Harries' attempt to pay a cheque for nine pounds into his account at Whitland – after it had been altered to the rather startling figure of £909. The cheque had been drawn by the missing John Harries, and when the clerk at the Whitland bank pointed out the discrepancy he informed the dismayed Ronald that the uncle's balance stood at only £123. The nephew had entered into a long and rambling explanation of how he had made expensive purchases for his uncle, including supplies of poultry food, a car tyre, and a couple of tractor tyres, as well as lending him a large sum in pound notes and cashing a number of cheques for him. To clear this up his uncle had given him the cheque altered to £909, to settle all arrears and moneys owing and leave sufficient for the purchase of a hay baler which uncle and nephew were to own jointly.

Capstick was inclined to say of this involved explanation what George Wilson had said when questioned about Ronald Harries towing his broken-down car to the gate of his farm : 'Not a word of truth in it.'

Thus far Capstick had proved Ronald Harries was a persistent liar, but lying did not make the man a murderer. Only the discovery of John and Phoebe Harries would prove that – or otherwise. While Scotland Yard men made inquiries in London arrangements were made for a comb-out of the countryside surrounding the Taff Valley, now being described as the Valley of Fear in some of the newspapers that had sent reporters to the area. This was because some of the local farmers had banded themselves to search for a possible murdering marauder. On the evening of 12 November these farmers and others met in the Gwalia Hall in St Clears and were addressed by the Chief Constable in both English and Welsh. They were asked to search their native valley thoroughly.

'Search your own farms first,' the assembly was told. 'Go over every inch of ground within a hundred yards of your roads and paths. Prod every soft patch of ground with rods. Examine every hedge, every gateway, and look for wheel marks and tyre tracks not made by your own vehicles. Sound every pond, ditch and stream. And let us know about every suspicious thing you find, no matter how slight. You will be helped by hand-picked police officers, every one of them a farmer's son. And when you have covered every foot of your own farms we'll start on the rest of the countryside. Sooner or later we'll find John and Phoebe Harries.'

Whatever these instructions and their final promise meant, those farmers rose from their seats knowing they were expected to look for two bodies, which meant the police were also bent on proving the fact of murder.

There were two hundred and fifty members of the local branch of the National Farmers' Union in the Gwalia Hall that night. 'Before the meeting was over,' Capstick said later, 'they had become the first officially constituted band of vigilantes ever known in Britain.'

In the next days fear roamed that valley – fear of what would be found, fear of what was loose and unknown. For now rumours were turning from Derlwyn and people were recalling that only months earlier an old woman had been murdered in her small cottage at Laugharne. Was there a compulsive killer stalking the Taff Valley? At night doors and windows were barred and bolted. Some farmers slept with shotguns within reach.

Capstick heard the rumours and discounted them. To him it was not insignificant that no one from Cadno had attended the Gwalia Hall meeting. The Yard men concentrated their attention on the big search, which was to be made on a Sunday, with men from five parishes assembled, each band under its own leader. Some crossed the streams and rivers in coracles, such as were used by the ancient Britons. They plumbed the water with long ash poles and paddles. Searchers beat their way in bad weather across hill and field and forest. Ditches and ponds were waded, bogs tramped by men bent double. A vast army of searchers scaled the shoulders of the Marros mountain. Later, troops combed the sand-dunes of broad Carmarthen Bay, while farmers on horseback took their sheepdogs to farther lonely places. In the village of Marros the search was directed by loud hailer near the war memorial. A mobile canteen served a thousand cups of hot tea to chilled searchers. But John and

Phoebe Harries were not found.

Capstick was then sure of one thing. He had to concentrate his search nearer Derlwyn, possibly where Ronald Harries was now living, at Cadno, his parents' farm. He was confirmed in this by the self-assured air the young farmer wore, almost as though he were enjoying a joke at the expense of the police. The farm was accordingly watched, day and night. It was at night that Capstick and Bill Heddon set up a device the former had been taught by Inspector Alf Dance years before in the Flying Squad. Alf Dance was the first Yard detective to be nicknamed Charlie Artful by the London underworld. Perhaps what Capstick did at Cadno shows why they both were given the name.

Lengths of black and green thread, that could not be seen in the dark, were secretly tied across every entry to Cadno Farm and its surrounding fields. On the Monday morning following the great search based on Marros, Capstick found some of his threads broken. They were threads he had set across an entry to what was known as Top Field, which adjoined the Pendine-Red Roses road. This was a field that was invisible from both the farm and the main road. It was triangular in shape, with bracken and brambles extending for thirteen yards near the farm gateway. Beyond a surface drain the field was planted with winter kale. Capstick asked Inspector Fox of the Carmarthenshire County Constabulary to have the field searched.

The police began their task near the drain, at a place where the bracken had been chopped down and some kale plants had been left lying with their roots exposed. At a depth of eighteen inches the police searchers uncovered a dark overcoat. Word was sent to Capstick, who shortly afterwards arrived in Top Field with the Chief Constable. They were watching the progress of the digging operation when a woman's clothed body was uncovered. This was removed and the digging continued to produce, below where the female body had been lying, the body of a clothed man. The skulls of both man and woman had been smashed by heavy blows.

Capstick stared at the evidence of murder. It was just before noon and the sun was trying without much success to shine through watery-looking clouds.

The Yard man still wanted to find the murder weapon

and when it was not found in the three-foot pit with the bodies he had a search made elsewhere on the farm. But this time the police drew blank. Ronald Harries was questioned again, cautioned, and arrested for the murders of John and Phoebe Harries. He protested that he was innocent.

Four days later a Tenby farmer named Laurie Evans arrived at Cadno to collect the cows, a tractor trailer, and a potato spinner that had been the property of the murdered farmer. It was while he was having trouble with the trailer that he trod on something hard in some undergrowth. He stooped and found he had stepped on a large hammer head. It had been pushed into the ground by its shaft. The hammer was shown to a man named Lewis who, Capstick had discovered, had loaned Ronald Harries a large hammer on the night when John and Phoebe Harries were murdered, the fatal Friday, 16 October.

'That's the hammer I lent Ron Harries,' Lewis said with no hesitation.

One other piece of evidence helped to complete Capstick's case. Curiously it was provided by that same George Wilson of Middlepool Farm who had vigorously denied being given a tow by young Harries. He and his wife, he told Capstick, had called at Cadno a few evenings before 16 October, though he couldn't be sure of the date. It was about eight o'clock when he saw Ronald, who told him, 'I've started to dig a well up in Top Field.' George Wilson had agreed that it was a good thing to have water for the Cadno fields.

Capstick's case was complete except for knowing when and where the crime had been committed. This was a surprise that was kept for the prosecution to offer at the trial, which opened at Carmarthen Assizes on 8 March 1954 and lasted for eight days. Mr Edmund Davies, QC, who led for the Crown, held the attention of everyone in court as he asked rhetorically, 'When?' and went on to give an answer.

'They were killed,' he said, 'between eight-forty-five pm on the Friday and eighty-thirty am on the Saturday. Certainly they were dead by eight-thirty am.'

The time when Ronald James arrived at Derlwyn.

Mr Davies continued, 'How? By Friday evening Harries had borrowed the weapon which killed them. He had a Land-Rover which could very conveniently become the necessary hearse to carry their bodies to the grave. Why? One motive was personal gain. He coveted the victims' car, their dairy stock and farm implements, and thought they had money in the bank. The two murders were born out of greed.'

Then the prosecution suggested that the prisoner had by some means induced his uncle and aunt to visit Cadno. That was the purpose of his visit on the Friday night. He had driven them there in the Land-Rover and taken them to the well-screened place where he had supposedly been digging a well. This meant that he had driven them to their grave and murdered them on the site. Capstick had found Land-Rover tyre tracks to support this claim.

On the last day of what had proved to be a sensational trial four thousand people crowded in the street outside the court building. The police had been compelled to erect crash barriers. Some of the spectators had camped beside them throughout a cold night.

When the jury that had sat listening to the evidence for more than a week retired they had only to consider one charge against the prisoner, the murder of John Harries. It was felt the prosecution did not have to charge the prisoner at that time with the murder of Phoebe Harries. They were absent for eighty-seven minutes before delivering their verdict of 'Guilty'.

When Harries appealed against the verdict the plea was dismissed, and Lord Goddard, then Lord Chief Justice, said in his statement from the chair, 'No one who had heard the case could have the slightest doubt that he was the killer. The case against him was overwhelming.'

The man who had made it overwhelming was John Capstick.

Thomas Ronald Lewis Harries was hanged at Swansea Prison. On the day he died Capstick was travelling from Scotland Yard to find a criminal wanted in another corner of Britain.

3 HIT AND RUN FAST

Sergeant Brennan was a New York cop in the days before the First World War. After years on the beat and later working at a desk he was put in charge of a section that trained new recruits to the Department. Someone called him the Rookies' Uncle. In one sense at least the name was justified. He took his teaching duties seriously and tried conscientiously to make his charges into cops who could act and think as they should in difficult circumstances.

They were days when the streets of New York, like those of every other major city on both sides of the Atlantic, were being changed by the growth of motor vehicle traffic. Brennan held some revolutionary ideas about cars.

'The time will come,' he told his class of rookies, 'when the automobile will be as important in police work as the man who drives it.'

It was this kind of statement from their instructor that produced smiles on the faces of his listeners. They had all been born in the horse and buggy era. They knew automobiles were beginning to crowd the thoroughfares, but it would be many years before horses disappeared from the streets, and even longer before the automobile could make any impact on police work and routine. Sergeant Brennan was to prove otherwise. Indeed, he was not only to surprise the doubters in his own class, but to demonstrate to his superiors that a new age of detective work had arrived.

As he made his way home on a June evening he had no idea that events were moving to provide him with an opportunity not only to justify his revolutionary views, but to ensure that his name would be remembered along with those of other men who achieved notable detective feats during their police careers.

A short while after Sergeant Brennan had arrived home, taken off his tunic and exchanged his boots for slippers, a horse-drawn buggy clip-clopped its way along Sixty-ninth Street, going west between Lexington Avenue and Park Avenue. The man holding the reins was a foreman employed by New York City's municipal street-cleaning department.

His name was John McHugh, and part of his work was to drive around the city at night to inspect the streets. It was an inspection tour for which he had little liking, and he was always glad when it was over. McHugh had found that night-time invited the drivers of some of the new automobiles to speed through the long straight streets.

In those days there were few traffic police. Traffic lights had not been invented as an urgent necessity. There was no accepted driving code for motorists. They weaved in and out of other traffic with as much ease as the driver's skill and good fortune permitted. But already the road hog had made his appearance although he had not yet been named.

It was one of these that had a fatal rendezvous with John McHugh that hot June night.

As the buggy driven by the foreman reached the corner of Park Avenue and Sixty-ninth Street a car driven at speed came from the rear. It could not pull up in time to avoid the buggy so the driver swerved, struck the horse-drawn vehicle a smashing blow, bounced away from the impact, and with a roar from its exhaust tore round a corner and vanished. Like the road hog, the hit-and-run driver had also arrived on the city scene.

The impact had thrown the smashed buggy on to its side and tossed McHugh on to the pavement as though he had been a rag doll. He had landed at the bottom of a flight of brownstone steps, unconscious. The horse had not even been thrown. The light shafts had snapped, the scared animal had jumped away, and when Officer John G. Dwyer, from the Seventieth Street Precinct, ran up after hearing the crash the animal was trying to get its feet free from the entangling reins.

Dwyer took charge of the horse and sent someone to summon aid in getting the injured McHugh to hospital. Unfortunately when the foreman was brought into the Presbyterian Hospital he was found to be dead.

The death was duly reported by Dwyer to the Police Department. The accident posed his superiors with a problem. The driver who had crashed into the buggy might be responsible for John McHugh's death. If so, he could legally be guilty of manslaughter. That unknown driver had to be found. His driving away was a challenge to the Police Department.

But where was he to be sought in a city with more than five million people? McHugh had died from his injuries before he could talk about the accident. So far as the police could learn there had been no witness to what had happened. At first glance it looked as though the driver responsible for McHugh's death had got clear away.

However, if there were no witnesses, there was the wreckage strewn across the street corner. It was all collected by Dwyer and those who helped him after the dead man's horse had been taken to a stable. The wreckage was held by the New York Police Department. It included not only the remains of the buggy, much of it smashed to matchwood, but also a collection of broken pieces of glass, patiently picked up and kept apart by Dwyer, who also noted stains in the roadway made by spilled fuel from the car's tank.

John Dwyer spent a long time over his report because the amount of fuel spilled had given him an idea. He enlarged upon it in his hand-written account of his findings. He said that, in his opinion, the hit-and-run car must have been seriously damaged in the accident, and the driver might well have been compelled to take it to a garage for immediate repairs.

His report was attached to a large envelope containing the twenty-one pieces of broken glass. When he handed the package to his superior he did not imagine that he had done anything that would help another member of the Department to make police history. In fact, Officer Dwyer went home and tried to forget the business of the accident for the few hours before he had to attend the formal inquest on the dead man.

However, while Dwyer was in bed asleep one of the cleaners in John McHugh's group of personnel began sweeping up the scene of the accident. This was done at an early hour in the morning before the busy streets filled. In those days horse droppings were swept up regularly, especially in hot summer weather, and that June was no colder than most New York enjoys. There was plenty of light when the crossing sweeper pushed his long-handled broom round the corner of Park Avenue and Sixty-ninth Street and saw something dark roll away in front of it. The dark object made no sound. He stooped and picked it up. What he had found was a small piece of hard rubber, no more than three inches in length and jagged along the sides. He put it in his pocket and later showed it to a policeman.

'Think it might have anything to do with that accident in which McHugh was killed?' he asked.

The patrolman fingered the broad sliver of rubber and shook his head.

'I'll hand it in and let someone else decide,' he said, taking out his notebook. 'But you'd better let me have your name and where we can contact you later, and you'd better give me the exact spot where you found it and the time.'

The piece of rubber and another brief report joined the envelope attached to Dwyer's first report. The wreckage of the buggy was collected with other refuse and junk. Twenty-one pieces of broken glass and that small scrap of rubber were all the police had to show that there had been an accident.

At a senior officers' conference someone said the scraps should be handed to one man who knew something about cars. That would be the best way to handle the situation. Let one man keep on the case.

'He'll need all the luck he can get,' it was agreed.

The question was who was the man to be. Several names were suggested, but the men's superior in each case claimed that he already was fully engaged in an important investigation. Then someone remembered Sergeant Brennan.

'John Brennan would be a good man for this inquiry,' it was claimed. 'Right now he's in the training school, and among his subjects is automobile recognition and identification.'

It was agreed that Sergeant John F. Brennan could be spared for a while from his rookies' classes to make inquiries about the hit-and-run car and driver. Accordingly, some hours later Sergeant Brennan found himself once more investigating an actual case that could involve a criminal, one who drove at reckless speed at a late hour in a car that had been damaged.

Brennan's first move on the case was to seek out Dwyer and talk to the patrolman.

'Any help you can give me,' he told Dwyer, 'will be appreciated. I've got a feeling this is going to be a test case for John Brennan.'

Dwyer grinned back at the amiable sergeant. He knew about Brennan's teachings and that any officer who had to go to court with a case involving a car preferred to have the sergeant's assurance that his facts would stand up when challenged by a defence counsellor.

'You've got little enough to start with, sergeant,' Dwyer said. 'Some bits of glass and a piece of chewed-up rubber.'

'Why do you say chewed up?' Brennan asked.

'Well, that's how it looked to me when I saw it. Chewed up or ripped off something.'

Brennan had another question for Dwyer. 'Would you say it might have been torn off a tyre that had hit something sharp while travelling fast? Something like the wheel hub of a buggy, Dwyer.'

A look of wonder came to Dwyer's broad homely face.

'You know, sergeant,' he nodded, 'it just might have been that. A wheel hub on McHugh's buggy.'

Satisfied that this small piece of theory did not appear faulty in the eyes of a police officer directly concerned wth the accident, Sergeant Brennan next gave his attention to a jigsaw puzzle with pieces of glass. He spread the twenty-one pieces on a broad sheet of paper. Some were convex and others concave and others again were of plain glass. The concave and convex lenses could be turned either way, but when he found tiny traces of soot in some of the small ridges in the glass against the convex surfaces he was sure he had a broken lens or lenses from lamps that burned oil.

He began trying to fit the pieces together. This was not at all easy because some of the edges were chipped and splintered and only in a few instances did he find he had a precise fit. It is said he worked at his jigsaw with the aid of a compass. When he was satisfied that he had created as full a pattern as possible with the concave-convex pieces of glass he found he could now

40

measure the size of the diameter of a car's headlamp. It was six inches.

Next he started on the pieces of plain glass. Using the same method as with the ridged and curved pieces of glass, he slowly built up a fresh pattern with the plain glass and was able to measure a larger diameter. Eight inches.

So he had two different lamps. One burned oil and one was a gas lamp.

The pieces of glass in their distinct patterns were stored on trays and he turned to the piece of rubber that certainly looked as though it had been chewed at the edges. By tracing it on paper and tracing the distinct curve of its shape, he found that he had what could be a piece of rubber from a four-inch car tyre. He sketched the proportions of a tyre with a four-inch tread.

Next he secured a magnifying glass and returned to his trays of glass pieces, which he examined minutely, finding tiny figures on some of the pieces of glass. To make the figures correspond and have meaning he had to rearrange a few of the pieces in the patterns he had made. He then found he had discovered a patent number, applying to one of the lenses.

At this stage he began to feel a growing excitement, and lost no time in calling at the New York Public Library. He referred his quest to the director in charge of the reference section containing volumes on established patents. After a good deal of research he traced a record of the number he had seen through his magnifying glass. It was a patent number that had been awarded to a glass manufacturer. The company was Macbeth Incorporated, with offices and factory in Pittsburgh.

He returned from the library certain that he had taken a real step forward. But now he wanted to discover the colour of the hit-and-run car. He could do so, he felt, by examining the smashed buggy for possible traces of paint. However, when he asked about the remains of the buggy it was to be told they had been collected by the garbage collectors. Instead of accepting partial defeat, Brennan started a hunt for those missing remains.

His zeal was rewarded by finding them, still awaiting collection for burning. Again his magnifying glass came into use, and on the left-hand shaft he discerned minute particles of a different colour of paint. It was grey. He also found some of the tiny grey paint specks caught in the unpainted splintered ends of the shaft, where it had snapped under the impact of the speeding car.

He returned with the broken shaft to the office where he worked and started to draft a letter to the Macbeth Company. He could do little until he received their reply. He realized that it was useless making inquiries at repair garages until he knew the model of car he was trying to trace. Dwyer's idea that the accident could have resulted in the car's fuel tank being damaged was certainly encouraging, but how far the hit-and-run driver could continue across the city depended on the amount of fuel in his tank and how bad was any leak that had been started.

The reply he received from the Macbeth Company was encouraging in at least two respects. It not only confirmed that the lamp had been manufactured by them, but it fixed the lamp as belonging to a model of car that was at least four years old. The company no longer made a headlamp with that type of lens, and had not done so since 1912.

Brennan now began checking on models that had used the earlier type of lamp made by the Macbeth Company. He not only went through the lists of automobiles he had compiled in his own study of the subject, but he went to showrooms and to secondhand car dealers.

He came to the firm conviction that the car which had smashed into McHugh's buggy was a 1909 Packard, Model 18, painted a medium grey shade. When he told his superiors they were frankly astounded. Some were even sceptical. But when Brennan produced the results of his research and inquiry and demonstrated how he knew the kind of car that had been involved in the accident scepticism gave place to genuine appreciation. John Brennan had demonstrated that logic applied to painstaking detective work earned a satisfactory result.

Instructions were given to the entire New York Police Department to inquire at repair garages about such a car as Brennan had named as the one they wanted. However, perhaps things had gone too smoothly for the persevering sergeant. Now he had to face the prospect of failure through no fault of his own.

Daily reports came in that such a 1909 Packard had been traced through information supplied by a garage, but none of them was the car Brennan sought. Either the repairs undertaken did not fit the wanted car or their owners had an alibi for the night of the accident or it could be proved the car had not been out of a garage on the day in question. It began to look very much as though Brennan's brilliant detective work would be for nothing, that the driver had left New York and vanished success-fully without leaving any trace.

John Brennan was a man with a dogged streak in him. He refused to believe that the car would not be traced eventually. He also made his views very clear that the search for the missing car should be extended. Because he was prepared to make him-self a nuisance he had his way. The search was extended. It at last reached Long Island City, where the owner of a repair garage recalled that such a grey 1909 Packard was being used as a self-drive hire in Yorkville. The hunt for the car now switched to Yorkville, and after a patient process of inquiry and elimination the plain-clothes men were left with one garage that was suspect. It was rumoured that such a Packard had been left there shortly before, but when the police made inquiries they were told by the foreman in charge that the car had been taken away two days previously.

The car had been in for repairs and these included fitting new lamps and fixing the fuel tank. The police were given the car's number and the name and address of its owner.

The man they now wanted to interview was Louis Casella, who had given his address as 113 East Seventy-fifth Street, New York City.

The new information was passed on to Brennan, who went to East Seventy-fifth Street and made inquiries at number 113 only to draw a blank. Louis Casella lived there, he was told, but he had left home without telling anyone where he was going. Again the sergeant had to retire and consider his next move. The people living at number 113 were certainly not inclined to be helpful.

He took to observing where letters delivered at the East Seventy-fifth Street house had been posted, and found that a number had the name Allenhurst, New Jersey franked across the stamps. He questioned the postmen who made deliveries in the street. They told him the letters from Allenhurst had only been arriving recently. Since, in fact, the grey Packard had left Yorkville.

43

Sergeant Brennan was once more a man hot on the trail of a man he wanted to question. He went to Allenhurst and began inquiries on his own, without announcing his arrival in the town to the New Jersey police. The work now was routine, calling at a list of garages he had obtained, but he was anxious that the man he wanted did not hear of the search and decamp.

After a couple a days he found a garage in which the car he was anxious to locate had been left. He checked the repairs that had been done in Yorkville, and then became a one-man stake-out, waiting for Louis Casella to show himself. Casella, as it turned out, was in no hurry, but when he did arrive and go to his car Brennan was tapping on the window before he had settled himself behind the wheel.

'Mr Louis Casella?' Brennan asked.

'Yes,' said the man in the car, frowning unpleasantly. 'What is this?'

'I'm a police officer and I'd like to ask you some questions – about your car.'

Louis Casella, a rotund man with an irascible manner and quick, darting eyes, remained behind the wheel of the grey Packard.

'All right,' he said, 'ask.'

His manner was defiant, and his defiance arose from the fact that he professed to have an alibi for the June night about which Brennan questioned him. The alibi was not one that impressed the sergeant who was a stickler for detail. But he did not have enough evidence with him in Allenhurst to justify arresting Casella. In addition, he wanted to be absolutely sure that he could prove this was the hit-and-run car, and no other.

With a mocking Casella watching him, he bent down over the wheel that, in his reckoning, was likely to be the one that had been gouged by the buggy's hub cap. He found a rough surface that seemed to have been smoothed over into which the piece of rubber picked up at the scene of the accident might fit. There was a small piece of the tyre surface hanging in a strip. Without allowing Casella to see what he was doing, he plucked this small piece of rubber from the tyre.

When he straightened his back he sighed.

'That all?' grinned Casella.

Brennan nodded and without saying anything walked out of the garage, well content to let the other man fool himself into believing he had tricked the police.

The sergeant returned to New York and called on an analytical chemist. He produced the two pieces of rubber, the one found at the scene of the accident, the other that he had torn off Casella's tyre.

'What I want to know,' he said, 'is if these strips of rubber are identical.'

The chemist stared at them. 'Tyre rubber, sergeant?' he asked.

'Yes.'

'Then what you really want to know is if these pieces are from tyres of the same make.'

'You convince me they are and I'll be a happy man,' Brennan told the other.

A couple of days later the chemist rang Brennan.

'The rubber pieces you left with me, Sergeant Brennan,' he reported, 'are virtually the same in composition and structure. They are certainly from tyres of the same make, and might even be from the same tyre.'

Brennan had his case. All he had to do now was demonstrate to his superiors that it was one that would hold up in court. Again he prepared a report and in his rounded and easily legible hand wrote:

> The automobile that struck the buggy in which Foreman McHugh was driving is a Packard, 1909, Model 18, grey with white stripes, nickel lamps, licence number 67388. It is owned by Louis Casella of 113 East Seventy-fifth Street, New York.
>
> I have traced this car to Deal's Garage, Allenhurst, New Jersey, and can state positively that it is the car of the collision.

His superiors passed on the report to the detective bureau, to whom he had to make a fresh report in person and answer direct questions in an interview. What Sergeant John Brennan that day told the grouped New York detectives made them stare at him with little short of awe. This case had been prepared by a man who spent his time teaching fresh recruits how to use their eyes when they were sent out on patrol in New York's Streets.

What Brennan had done was teach the detective bureau how to investigate accidents involving cars and hit-and-run drivers.

He was told, 'We'd better get hold of copies of the garage's receipted bills for those repairs, Sergeant Brennan. Perhaps it would be best if you did this, with Detective Cousins to help you.'

Brennan hid a smile. The detective bureau didn't want him to foul up their work now that it had become strictly routine and any slip-up at the last minute could be laid at their door.

So John Brennan and Ted Cousins arranged to make the last check-up together. When they returned to Center Street the required copies of the bills paid by Louis Casella for repairs to his grey Packard were in Cousins' pocket.

Brennan was greeted with smiles in the detective bureau. However, those smiles slipped when detectives sent to arrest Casella came back empty-handed.

'He's left and no one can say where he's gone,' they reported.

Apparently Casella had been scared by Brennan's appearance in Allenhurst and the nature of the questions he had put to the Packard's owner.

'Now we've got to scour the city to find him,' Ted Cousins informed the sergeant.

'Did he take his car?' Brennan asked.

Cousins shook his head. 'No, that's still over in Jersey. Could be he's left by train and won't be back.'

But Sergeant Brennan was capable of making up his own mind when told enough facts. He didn't believe Casella had left for parts unknown without his car. The man had been ready for Brennan with a loose-knit alibi, but that was enough to show that he wasn't the type to run away – except perhaps at the wheel of a car. Wherever he was he was without his car.

The way Brennan saw it, Casella's confidence had been badly shaken, but the man still felt he could beat the police, and most likely he had been taking the next logical step, as he had prepared an alibi in advance. The next logical step, as Brennan realized, was to approach a lawyer and get some useful advice about what could be done to save himself.

If his lawyer was a good one he would be bound to tell Casella there was nothing he could do if the car was proved to be his. He would need a much better alibi than the one he had offered Brennan.

So again Sergeant John Brennan behaved in a manner in which he would have advised his class of rookies to behave. He returned to East Seventy-fifth Street and began making fresh inquiries, but not at number 113. He called at a number of stores until he found a trader who could tell him the name of the lawyer used by Louis Casella when the owner of the grey Packard had legal matters that required handling.

Next Brennan found this lawyer's address and then went to the building and made further tactful inquiries about a man answering to the description of Louis Casella. The superintendent of the building was certain that no such man had visited the lawyer's office in the past few days.

This didn't look too good for the hunch Brennan was playing. But he was of a firm mind and decided he had to go all the distance to finish this case in his own way. It had become a matter of personal pride with him. After all, he had to return to his classes and face the stares of young recruits who would be expecting him to back up his words with action. He had preached that proof was better than theory.

Again John Brennan became a one-man stake-out, as he had in Allenhurst. Throughout a boiling hot day he remained standing and sweating in a doorway, observing the entrance to the building holding the lawyer's offices. When passers-by showed suspicious interest in the unknown loiterer he changed his observation post. He moved a short way down the street to a telephone kiosk, and held the door slightly open so that the strong sunlight hit the glass at an angle that produced a reflected glare and no one passing would see inside.

A very warm summer's afternoon was well advanced when Brennan's incredible patience was rewarded by sight of a familiar figure that was making for the building the sergeant had been watching.

Before Louis Casella could enter the building where his lawyer was waiting he felt a hand on his shoulder and spun around angrily.

'You!' he exclaimed.

' Me,' Brennan nodded.

Louis Casella was not behind the wheel of a car. He went quietly after hearing the words that informed him he was under arrest.

4 THEY CALLED HIM
THE PANTHER

About four years after Sergeant Brennan in New York returned to lecture rookies on police procedures in dealing with crime after the successful conclusion of his hunt for Louis Casella, a group of young detectives sat in a room of Scotland Yard, in London, to receive a similar lecture on the methods employed by various criminals.

The lecture was given by Arthur Fowler Neil, who had specialized in what in 1920 was termed the *modus operandi* method, or identifying a known criminal by the way in which he operated in committing a crime.

Just before Brennan caught Casella, Neil had successfully trailed and captured that multiple murderer, George Joseph Smith, notorious for his 'Brides in the Bath' murders. But it was not the *modus operandi* of the ingenious but callous Smith that Neil discussed that day. He chose the criminal activities of a burglar he had captured a good many years before, in his earlier days as a detective. This man had been known as the 'Panther' by his associates in the underworld of London in the early years of the present century, the period in which he had outwitted the police.

'No more suitable name could have been given him,' said Neil years later, after he had retired as a detective superintendent and one of Scotland Yard's famous original 'Big Four'. In 1920 the young detectives listened with a mixture of awe and admiration to the man lecturing. Neil, to them, was a man who had done it all. He had started as a London copper on an East End beat and he had risen to eminence in the Criminal Investigation Department. Moreover, these young detectives knew him as a rare man of courage. Neil's record showed that he had not been afraid to tackle a gunman with his bare hands or dive into the Thames to capture an escaping prisoner or mix in with a gang of toughs when on his own. He was one of the old-time stalwarts of the CID who had helped to hammer it into its modern shape after a World War, and in the process had created a living legend.

He was one of the Yard detectives who had taught the tricks of *modus operandi* to the first Charlie Artful, Alf Dance. Inspector Dance of the Flying Squad, who served under men like Nutty Sharpe and Bob Fabian, had later passed them on to men such as John Capstick, and so kept a legend alive and growing.

When Neil first encountered the Panther he was a detective sergeant in a division of South London that included the Peckham and Camberwell districts. The Panther was a burglar and a specialist. His speciality was jewellers' shops, and he made it a point never to work with a partner. He was what would be called these days a loner. He planned his jobs alone, operated alone, and shared none of the proceeds. This was the man who at the turn of the century began what was virtually a one-man crime wave.

Referring to the burglar's success in breaking into jewellers' shops and getting away undetected, Neil said, 'Before I came across him there had been quite a number of these places broken into and robbed at night.'

Twenty years later he told his audience of young detectives how the Panther operated. First, he made sure that the premises he was about to break into had two features – a projecting frontage and above this a flat roof. The latter was essential because the nimble burglar had a long rope ending in a grappling-iron. He would throw the grappling-hook on to the roof and when the rope was taut climb up it. Once on the roof he drew the rope up after him. Thus there was no obvious breaking into a shop from the street.

Among his tools he had a saw for cutting through the bolts securing a roof light. With the roof light open he secured the grappling-iron to the edge of the open space and dropped the rope through it. After that he climbed down the rope into the shop below. Undisturbed, he took from the stock in the shop any article that seized his fancy, then climbed back on to the roof, removed the rope and shut the roof lift, and at a suitable moment returned to the deserted street by his rope. A flick and a tug and the grappling-iron came free. He caught it before it chinked against the pavement, wrapped the rope around his body under his coat, and walked away, presumably content with the night's takings.

What made the Panther a specialist was the care and patience he brought to his criminal activities. Neil underlined this for his hearers when he explained : ' It did sometimes occur – although we did not know it at the time – that he could not remove the roof light bars the first night, and in such circumstances he would replace everything almost as he found it and return the next night.' As a specialist jewel thief he had one constant hunger – for diamonds.

When at work the Panther wore a stockinette mask over his face. He dressed entirely in black, and was sufficiently nimble to climb without risk and to be able to crouch in an incredibly small space. In more modern times such a man would have made a first-class wartime commando. Sometimes he was on the roof of a single-storeyed jeweller's shop or actually in the shop when a patrolling constable peered upwards and through the window and tried the door. The constable saw and heard nothing. The Panther was as undetectable as a shadow against a black background and as silent. Only when the constable had moved on and his footsteps receded did the Panther return to activity.

This was the elusive criminal known to be operating on Neil's ' patch ' when he came to South London. It wasn't long before some ex-convicts known to him took the chance to get in touch with the formidable detective who spoke their own language. Either they wanted to trade news or sought reassurance that they were not going to be charged with jobs they hadn't handled. There was a public-house near Camberwell Green called the Father Redcap by certain of its habituées where Neil would meet anyone who wanted to talk to him. One day he received word that a known criminal would be there expecting him at a certain time. Neil arrived to find the man talking to a smartly dressed young woman. Neil was introduced to her and then the man who had sent word to Neil said, 'I'll leave you two to-gether,' and before walking away winked at the detective.

'Well?' Neil said to the young woman, who was looking at the tall, well-built detective with anything but friendliness in her manner.

'I want you to know I don't like cops,' she said.

If she thought her bluntness would startle the detective she was disappointed. Neil grinned as though he had heard a favour-ite joke and asked mildly, 'Well, why have anything to do with me?'

'It suits my purpose,' she said spitefully.

Neil said nothing. As he told his listeners at Scotland Yard, 'When a woman speaks like that there is some underlying motive, and I have always made it an iron rule to keep silent and let them get on with the talking.'

On this occasion when she received no response from Neil the woman invited him to have a drink and he accepted. As she handed him a brimming glass of beer she said with a return of her former viciousness, 'I wish I could poison it!'

Neil raised his glass and drank. When he put it down he said, 'Cut out the rough stuff and get to business. I've a lot to do.'

Then he received a surprise. The woman's manner changed and became eager as she leaned towards him to ask, 'You want the man doing all these jewellers' shops?' The expression on her face registered a mixture of anger and mockery. 'He'd still beat the crowd of you – if I let him. But I'm not going to!'

Arthur Neil realized what this meeting was all about. A jealous woman wanted to take her own style of revenge. A few hours later she might regret her impulsiveness, but at the moment hurt pride led her to inflict a severe wound on a man who had turned away from her.

'I want revenge,' she told the silent Neil. Then she began to justify herself. She admitted she was a criminal who had been attracted to the Panther. He had tired of her and found another woman whose charms were more appealing. She ended by say-ing, 'I can tell you where you can put your hands on him tonight!'

That was when Neil broke his silence. He learned that the

Panther was planning to break into a large jewellers' shop that night in the Camberwell Road, but even more important to Neil was a description of the Panther given to him by the angry woman. When Neil and two other plain-clothes men took up positions near the jewellers' shop after dark the detective was certain he would know the elusive burglar when he came upon him. Up to that time no London police officer had been given a recognizable description of this phantom of the underworld. Neil had also briefed the constable patrolling that part of the Camberwell Road on night beat.

'Let him get to the place,' were Neil's instructions. 'As soon as he gets outside tackle him. We'll be covering both sides. He's almost certain to cut up rough; so you'll have help.'

As Neil said wryly many years later, 'So much for our plans, but they didn't fit in with those of the Panther!'

The wily crook must have been hidden and watching, and a good time later Neil learned that on this night the Panther had altered his intended time of breaking and entering. He was actually masked and inside the shop selecting what he wanted from its stock when the constable first appeared. Neil and his men were concealed not far away. The constable passed on. When he returned, acting as though uninterested in the jewellers' premises, Neil heard a sudden shout and the detectives broke from cover. He saw the constable on the ground. Neil turned to tackle a fast-running figure, but the man swerved and was out of reach, running with a speed neither Neil nor his men could match.

The time was just after midnight.

When the detectives reached the constable they found him lying unconscious and bleeding from a large gash on the side of the head. The Panther had smashed a large American steel-cutting ratchet in the man's face. Had the constable not been wearing his helmet his brains would have been scattered on the pavement.

The wounded man was taken to hospital and recovered slowly, but not to go back into police service. He was a permanent casualty of the grimly waged war on crime. He was declared unfit for service and retired with a pension.

Now Neil had a personal reason for cutting short the career

of a criminal who had proved himself violent to the point of being murderous. He went to his superior, Chief Inspector Fox, who was to make police history a few years later, when he caught the Stratton brothers, Alfred and Albert, charged them with a murder in Deptford, and later heard them convicted at the Old Bailey on the evidence of a thumbprint found on a rifled cash-box – the first time fingerprint evidence had been accepted in an English court of law.[1] Fox agreed to raid a house in a Camberwell back street whose address Neil had given him. Neil had been told the address by the woman wanting revenge. The house was near the Surrey Canal, and was divided into several flats. The Panther's mother and sister lived in a ground-floor flat in the front of the house, the Panther at the rear. There was a way of unlatching the front door of the house when one knew how. Neil knew how.

Neil and another man entered the house at two in the morning, while Chief Inspector Fox and another detective kept watch outside. Neil silently unlatched the door of the Panther's bedroom and began to open it. He had a momentary vision of the half-undressed crook rising from a sitting position on the side of a bed, and then the desperate man was throwing himself at the intruder. But without a heavy weapon in his hands the Panther had more than met his match. Neil readily closed with him and the two men fell struggling to the floor, Neil pinning the other down. Reinforcements arrived, and within minutes the prisoner was being marched to a cell in a police station.

Neil's task was only partially completed. He still had to recover, if he could, jewellery worth fifteen hundred pounds, including several valuable diamond rings. Neil believed that, because the Panther was a loner, he would not have told anyone about his recent haul. The only person who would share his knowledge would be the fence who paid him for the proceeds of the jewel robbery. But when he had searched the Camberwell house without finding the missing jewellery Neil decided the Panther's mother had a reason for sneering at what she mockingly called the cleverness of the police. She used the word several times, and on each occasion laughed as though enjoy-

[1] See 'The Fight for Fingerprints' in the author's *Stories of Famous Detectives* (Arthur Barker Ltd).

ing a secret joke.

'You've got him, but not the stuff,' she sneered, 'and you never will get it.'

Neil waited until the mother was in another room, then he questioned the daughter, who seemed less callous and even somewhat subdued. He asked her if she knew where the stolen property was concealed and she said in a barely audible whisper, 'No.' However, her eyes flashed quickly towards a pouffe, or hassock, by the fender. Neil had the mother brought back before he cut open the hassock with a penknife. 'I pulled out the stuffing. There were large lumps of wool, wadding, flock, and many sorts of packing, including lumps of tightly screwed-up tissue and coloured paper', Neil told that class of detectives in 1920.

'In about five minutes I had a good-sized heap in front of me, and it looked as though I had drawn a blank. Obviously my Sherlock Holmes deductions were at fault. I glanced at the elder woman. Her face was deathly white. I saw her look at the screwed-up paper in my hand. Even then I didn't know. To cover my disappointment I started to unscrew the paper. Then the secret hit me between the eyes. In my hands lay four beautiful diamond rings.'

Neil told the young detectives listening to him that in that hassock, concealed in screwed-up pieces of paper made to look like natural filling, he found jewellery worth eight thousand pounds, including two large Brazilian diamonds worth at that time about five hundred pounds each – which could be five thousand pounds today.

The Panther received five years' imprisonment when he came to trial. Neil thought the man had vanished from his life, like a good many other criminals he had caught. But he was wrong. More than five years later, when fingerprints had become valuable clues for any detective, another series of burglaries had Scotland Yard baffled for a time. They were not confined to one district, but extended throughout London, on both sides of the river. Again the indications were that a lone cracksman, to use a new word of the time, was responsible.

Issued by the Metropolitan Police was a periodical publication called *Special Release Notices*. The information it contained was confidential, for it listed details about convicts released from penal servitude. It was when Arthur Neil sat in his office glancing through one of these publications that he noticed the name of the man known to him as the Panther. It was a piece of information he kept against the time when a burglary bearing the *modus operandi* of the Panther occurred in what Neil thought of in that day as his 'manor'.

As it turned out, he was luckier than he could have hoped. The Panther's known enjoyment of female companionship resulted in Neil catching a glimpse of him talking to a colourful blonde. The detective took a mental photo of the woman, and next morning was glad of it. That night a premises was burgled on Neil's 'manor' and again the Panther had become his quarry, for the crime bore the familiar hallmark of a man who wouldn't and perhaps couldn't change his ways.

Neil knew that the Panther was a ticket-of-leave man, which meant that since leaving prison he had to report regularly to the police in the area where he lived. However, he was almost never at the address he had given, which, for all the police knew, might have been an accommodation one, for the Panther was only required to make his report to the police once a month. So instead of wasting time looking for the Panther, who could almost smell policemen by a kind of criminal's instinct, Neil looked for the blonde. She was eventually seen in the Old Kent Road and trailed to a house in Walworth Road. Cautious inquiries were made about her. She was living in the house ostensibly as a married woman, and her husband was understood locally to be a smartly dressed character who was employed by a firm in the City of London.

'I kept my knowledge to myself and waited for my moment to arrive,' Neil informed the young detectives he was lecturing at Scotland Yard. 'It came six weeks later.'

He was having a cup of tea at eight o'clock in the morning when a constable from the Borough Police Station, not far from Southwark Cathedral, rang the front door bell and told him he was wanted urgently. That was in the days before detectives had telephones in their own homes. Neil hurried back with the constable and was informed that a jewellers' shop had been raided in the night and the thief had vanished with a haul worth thousands. Neil asked for details, and as he listened he recognized the burglar's *modus operandi*. 'The details of the job,' he said, 'were just what I was expecting.'

The crook had climbed across several roofs by means of a rope fitted with a grappling-iron, and had dropped into the shop in the way that was stamped as the Panther's handiwork. Iron bars had been cut and the best stock, worth about five thousand pounds, taken from the showcases. However, the owner of the shop lived on the premises at the back and something had roused him that night. He had gone into his shop and the Panther had heard him approaching. The thief had left hurriedly by the shop's door, and he was able to do this because he had taken the precaution of inserting a skeleton key in the lock as soon as he reached the shop. The Panther was a skilled professional burglar and made sure he had a way of escape before he devoted his attention to gathering loot.

But on this night his luck had almost run out. He had no time to collect his rope and grappling-iron, and as he turned to run up the street the owner had a brief glimpse of his face in the light from a street-lamp.

Everything Neil heard confirmed his belief that the Panther was the man who had narrowly escaped a few hours before. His superior at that time, Chief Inspector Godley, agreed with him that they should visit the blonde who lived in Walworth Road. When she opened the door to them Neil saw the Panther standing at the top of the stairs at the end of the narrow hall. He pushed past the woman and told the Panther to come down. The man, rather to Neil's surprise, complied. Then Neil told him in formal terms that he had reason to believe the other had broken into a jewellers' shop in the early hours of that morning in the Newington Causeway.

The Panther grinned. 'Where's your proof?' he asked, a man very sure of himself. 'You can't find the stuff, and besides, I have an alibi.'

Neil told him he would have to come to the police station, and the woman went to call a cab. She climbed in with them. Neil sat holding his prisoner's wrist. Godley was on the other side of the Panther, and the woman opposite. It was a horse-drawn hansom cab, and as soon as it was moving the blonde threw herself on the three men and began hitting Neil and Godley. The cab had swung into Newington Causeway when Neil, busy fending off the bright-haired virago, felt a sharp pain in his forearm. The Panther had bitten him savagely in an effort to force Neil to release his hold. Neil told his audience that he was sure, had he done so, the Panther would have killed him.

The cab reached the police station with the Panther's teeth still in Neil's arm and Neil's firm fingers still round the Panther's wrist, gripping hard.

As soon as the door flaps of the overflowing hansom were off Neil's knees he struck the Panther in the stomach with a violent jab of his left knee. The man collapsed, but inside the police station again became violent. It took several constables to restrain him even after he had been handcuffed. In the meantime Neil had had his bleeding arm bound with his own handkerchief. He returned to question the violent and angry prisoner.

'What have you got in your right hand?' he asked, nodding to the hand clenched in the prisoner's lap.

The Panther raised his hands to his face.

'Stop him!' Neil shouted.

Just in time the prisoner was prevented from thrusting a piece of paper into his mouth. The paper was taken from him only after another struggle in which it took six policemen to hold down the man who had been defeated for the second time by Arthur Neil. Neil took the small piece of much-creased paper to a window, watched by the angry gaze of the Panther. Smoothed out, the paper revealed a collection of letters and numbers. After staring at them for some moments the detective smiled. He knew why the prisoner was so desperately anxious to destroy the piece of paper. It was evidence of the kind Neil needed. The letters and numbers read as follows:

'GR 50. GW 30. DRS 50. DRH 25. DRHH 60. SW 30.'

They were, as Neil had suddenly realized, what he later called the Panther's 'private tally' for his receiver. He took the list to the jeweller who had been robbed. The list coincided with the articles of jewellery stolen. GR 50, for example, meant simply fifty gold rings; GW 30, thirty gold watches; DRS 50, fifty single-stone diamond rings; DRH 25, twenty-five diamond rings, hoop; DRHH 60, sixty diamond rings, half-hoop; SW 30, thirty silver watches.

'But,' Neil admitted ruefully later, 'I had, as I had done more than five years earlier, arrested him too soon!'

For Neil had the list, but not the stolen articles. They had still to be found. Neil was still searching when the Panther again stood in the dock and heard himself sentenced to seven years' penal servitude.

Neil had turned the house in the Walworth Road inside out, even unfastening the flock in the mattress and sifting through it, but he did not recover a single ring.

'The Panther had beaten me,' he confessed.

It was many years afterwards that he learned what happened to the large haul of stolen jewellery, and his informant was the same blonde who had been posing as the Panther's wife in Walworth Road and who had thrown herself at the detectives in the hansom cab. The reason she told Neil was that, upon his release from prison the second time, the susceptible crook had again given his favours to another pretty face.

'Do you remember,' she asked Neil, 'there were six metal meat covers on the dresser? Well, you looked under four of them, but the two large ones covered the swag. It was done up in four large silk handkerchiefs, and was hung on a hook suspended in a pear-shaped bundle. The bundles were covered over by the two large pewter covers. If you had lifted them –'

She shrugged, making a grimace.

Neil had not lost his interest with the passage of years.

'Where did the stuff go?' he asked her.

She hesitated before making another grimace. 'Well, you can't do anything now and there's no evidence and only my word,' she reminded him. It was yet another occasion when Neil kept silent, waiting for what she would tell him.

She went on, 'When you had gone I cleared off with it to my people in Liverpool. It was kept in a box until he came out, and to this day my people don't know. When he came out I took him all the stuff, just as he had knocked it off – and then three months afterwards he left me for another woman. That's why I'm now telling you the truth about where all that swag went.'

But the real victory was Neil's. The Panther did not go back to his rope and grappling-iron routine. His days as a roof-top crook were over. His *modus operandi* was too well known. Within a short while the country was at war with Germany and during hostilities the man who had been the Panther vanished, perhaps to die on a field in Flanders, while Neil was travelling the length and breadth of England securing evidence that would later hang the ' Brides in the Bath ' murderer.

5 KILLERS IN
VELVET MASKS

Just before the Riviera Express was due to leave the Gare de Lyon in Paris on a midsummer night in 1921, three men arrived on the platform where the train waited and swung aboard. Seconds afterwards the train pulled out of the station and headed south.

The three men had purposely left boarding the train till the last moment because the carriages of all the coaches save the first class were crammed with holiday-makers on their way to the Riviera sunshine. They had no wish to spend dragging minutes being watched by eyes that would later remember them.

As the train sped through the southern suburbs of the French capital the three men made their several ways down the train. Each stood in the corridor smoking, ready to avert his face whenever someone passed. That was a precaution insisted upon by the leader of this odd trio.

But then the leader had come with some odd equipment in his pocket – three velvet masks. The very last requirement of anyone travelling to the heat of the Mediterranean, where most of the people on that packed train looked forward to acquiring a suntan that would make the long journey to the sea worth while. Equally, it could be claimed, the average person going to the Riviera for a holiday had very small use for a gun. The three late arrivals had brought guns with them. The reason was not difficult to understand when their secret was shared. None of the three intended going as far as Provence and its azure sea. They were not even going to Lyon, where the train was scheduled to stop. They had planned to be back in Paris the next morning. With their pockets well lined, they hoped.

It was not until the express was running through the vineyards of Burgundy under a bright moon that the three men found the hands of their watches pointing to the agreed rendezvous hour. They started sauntering through the coaches until they were together. The leader took the slips of velvet with eye gaps cut in them from his pocket and gave a couple to his companions.

'We'd better check the guns – just in case,' he said quietly, keeping his voice down.

A few minutes later their took their positions. A compartment door was slid back. Sleepy eyes opened wide with shock at the sight of the masked man holding the gun.

'Don't make a sound,' said the intruder, waving his weapon, 'or I may have to use it. Now, your money, jewels – rings and brooches and earrings – and don't make me ask twice.'

The gun was brandished again. The hold-up man collected the modest wealth and pieces of jewellery of a group of frightened and intimidated people whose holidays he had ruined. As he backed to the door he had a parting word of warning.

'No one is to leave this compartment for the next hour. Unless he wants trouble.'

There was a last flourish with the hand holding the gun, light touched shadowed eyes in the mask and polished them momentarily with a false glitter, and then the door slid open and shut and the masked man with a gun was gone, like a phantom vanishing from a nightmare. The process of relieving the bemused and tremulous holiday-makers of money and gems continued smoothly while the train plunged through Nuits Saint-Georges and headed for Chagny. The holiday-makers could do nothing. The menace of the gun held them in their seats, especially if there were children in a carriage.

It was a carefully planned hold-up, operated while the train was at maximum speed, and any field worker who was up late that night and saw the flame-shot smoke drifting in the moonlight might have felt he had reason to envy the lucky ones aboard that racing train. He had no reason to imagine that an incredible drama was taking place as he watched, still less to imagine that murder was about to be committed above those humming steel wheels.

The hitch in the hold-up plans came when the door of a first-class compartment slid back to reveal two French Army officers trying to sleep. They had the compartment to themselves. One opened his eyes slowly, then jerked upright at what he saw. The low-wattage lamp in the ceiling of the compartment shone over the blue-black shape of an automatic in the grubby hand of a masked man. Behind him lurked another. From behind the mask covering the face of the first bandit came words gruffly spoken.

'Your money, messieurs.'

The second officer was sitting upright. He saw his travelling companion surrender his wallet to the outstretched left hand of the nearer bandit. He wore the insignia of a lieutenant and his name was Carabelli. He was a man with no wish to hand over his money meekly to the first person who asked for it, even if that person held a gun on him. He sprang up from where he was sitting and snatched at the weapon in the masked man's fist.

It was an abrupt and unexpected movement, and it took the bandit, who had just collected a wallet that felt well stuffed with notes, by surprise. The masked man half turned, but it was the wrong move. It helped Carabelli to grab the gun and wrench it from surprised fingers.

Carabelli pushed the gun's muzzle against the pale throat under the mask.

'Now you listen to me,' he said sternly.

The chances were that his intrepid action would have beaten the crooks had not the man on guard in the corridor looked in and been shocked in turn at how the tables had been swiftly turned. He threw back the door, wide, and pointed his own gun at the now armed lieutenant who was still covering the helpless bandit. Carabelli had only time to glance at the masked new-comer and then a gun exploded. It was not the weapon in the hand of the lieutenant. The shot was barely heard elsewhere in the train over the rattling sound of the hurrying wheels.

Lieutenant Carabelli dropped the gun he held and collapsed on the floor, his body rocking to the motion of the swaying train. His companion gave a cry and leaned over him.

'My God,' he exclaimed in a strangely hushed tone. 'You've murdered him!'

The two bandits said nothing. They backed out and shut the

door. The third member of the hold-up team, who had been covering the rear of the coach, came hurrying up.

'What's wrong?' he demanded. A couple of sentences told him all he needed to know.

'This is where we pull out,' he decided. There was no time for argument. He reached for the communication cord that connected with the locomotive's automatic braking system and tugged it down.

The brakes of the express screamed and the entire train jolted before slowing, with the coaches bumping one another down the entire length. At once shouts rose from the packed compartments, a good many of which had been visited by the masked hold-up men. Now the train was drawing to a steam-hissing stop there was very patently no time to be lost if the bandits wished to make their escape.

One of them wrenched open a door and dropped beside the track, screened from the moon's light by the snaking length of the train. He crossed the up track with the other two close at his heels. The three climbed a low embankment and vanished on the far side. With them went fifty thousand francs in holiday money – other people's.

Behind them they left the steaming and snorting train, prone in the night like some paralysed mastodon, while officials ran to discover why the express had been stopped so dramatically. The communication cord was traced to the compartment where Captain Morel was supporting the head of an unconscious lieutenant who was dying.

Some sort of order was urged out of the nightmare of chaos and the outraged and vociferous holiday-makers were ushered back to their compartments. The train's wheels turned again and the express that had plunged into tragedy was run as far as the next station. There the train waited while Carabelli was removed and taken to a hospital at Châlon-sur-Saône. Before doctors could do more than administer a pain-killing drug the lieutenant had died.

Meanwhile the express continued through the night towards Lyon and Nice with a cargo of passengers for whom sleep was very nearly impossible, while the telephone lines betwen Châlon and Paris hummed with agitated voices delivering information and reports, instructions and confirmation, until dawn wiped the last shadows from the vineyards of Burgundy.

Some hours after dawn a frowning detective sat in his office reading some of those reports that had been hurriedly typed out for him. He was the chief of the Special Brigade, and as he read he frowned in some perplexity, for Brigadier Mettefeu was finding a good deal of discrepancy and many minor contradictions in these first reports of statements made to local police by passengers of a Riviera train that had been held up at gunpoint. But Mettefeu did know that three masked men had been concerned in the daring robbery, though the mask of one had apparently become loosened due to the sweat pouring down his face on a hot night and some of the passengers were able to give an account of what his features looked like.

Mettefeu knew why he had those reports. The bandits must have joined the train at the Gare de Lyon, where it had left promptly on time at five minutes to eight. So the chances were they were Paris criminals. They were certainly violent and had gone armed. Mettefeu believed the chances were they would have police records if he could establish their identities. That was what he was expected to do – discover who these men from Paris who had committed murder were and collect enough evidence of their crime to make them stand trial.

Mettefeu was an outstanding French detective of his day, but that July morning when he sat reading the first accounts of the murder on the Riviera Express he was faced with a case that, before it was over, would be reported in all the civilized countries of the world.

His first act was to call a conference with other members of his Special Brigade. At this meeting he gave them the news and briefed them on what he wanted them to do in Paris while he was in Burgundy. He placed particular stress on criminal *dossiers* being checked for known violent thieves who had been released from prison and who might have schemed and operated such a daring crime. Then he left for Burgundy with a couple of his detectives. He began his search for clues from, as near as he could tell, the place where the express had slowed down. The railway line was searched and inquiries were made in several small villages not far from it. In one he was told of a fire that

E   65

had been lit in the early morning near the old cemetery at Nolay, which was not far across country from Chagny.

Mettefeu went there, found the remains of a recent fire, and he and his men sifted the ashes. They found the scorched and charred remnants of strips of velvet that fitted some of the descriptions Mettefeu had read in Paris. They also came upon discarded leather pocket wallets that had been taken from travellers and emptied. A good many papers had been burned. These had presumably been personal documents and letters taken from the discarded wallets. The Paris detectives collected all fragments that might be useful later, placed them in a bag, and walked from the fire-blackened wall of the graveyard.

Mettefeu decided the most likely direction to turn in now was north, heading back to Paris. In this he was proved right when one of his men who had been checking at local railway stations returned to inform him that three men had caught an early train from the station at Nolay. The train was a westbound one, and the three men had bought single tickets to Etang. Unfortunately the sleepy man in the ticket office had not bothered to look at these early passengers very closely. Earlier he had been wide awake, shocked at the news that had been flying down the line about a shooting on the Riviera Express and a dead man being taken to Châlon.

He told the detective asking questions that it was nearly five o'clock when he sold the tickets to Etang. Asked to make an effort to recall any detail about them, however small, he said, 'They all had muddy boots.' It wasn't much, but it fitted the few facts Mettefeu had. The bandits who had left the train in a hurry had crossed a number of muddy fields. It had been muddy in the Nolay cemetery. They must therefore have had mud on their boots when those tickets to Etang were bought at nearly five o'clock.

On the other hand, Mettefeu recognized the fact that the boots of any field workers at that hour in the morning, before the night's dew had dried out, would be muddy. But at least Etang and muddy boots joined together in the beginning of a chain of circumstances. At Etang he discovered the next link in the chain. Inquiry here produced a description of three men, still with muddy boots, who had gone on to Nevers, a good step on the way back to Paris. In Nevers, again, the three men had been observed. They had called at a café for breakfast and then gone to Montargis, almost due north of Nevers on the main road south from Fontainebleau.

By this time Mettefeu was convinced the trio was making its way back to Paris. He used up valuable time checking that they had journeyed to Charenton, which is a suburb to the south-east of the French capital between the Seine and the Bois de Vincennes. What interested Mettefeu was that at Charenton was the eastern terminus of a Métro underground line that could be taken to drop the wanted men almost anywhere in the city. To arrive at Charenton was to find himself at a temporary dead end.

Back in Paris the real work began, but it was work the Special Brigade was geared to undertake. Indeed, this was the kind of investigation that had brought the Brigade into existence. It operated with a minimum of its movements restricted by red tape. Mettefeu had been met on his return with the news that the files his men had consulted had produced no names worth checking. He had no starting point other than the statements of the passengers on the train. These had offered only two firm facts he could use. All three had been young men, under thirty if the passengers were to be believed, and one had been a dandy. His clothes were neat but cut with extravagant sharpness. He had worn pale gloves.

At a fresh conference Mettefeu told his Brigade members, 'We've now got to comb out the cafés and dance-halls from Montparnasse to Montmartre.'

The Brigade went to work and for Mettefeu this became the waiting period that was hard on the nerves, especially as the French press, which at that time liked to consider it was the most free in the world to comment on police and ordinary citizen alike, filled pages with wild theories about the Riviera Express murder. Because Mettefeu had not performed a miracle he was criticized, and through him the Special Brigade. Fortunately for him, Mettefeu had a thick skin. He gave no Press conferences, but he kept his men working late.

It was a man making routine checks in Montmartre who got the first useful lead. He had talked to a young woman named

Lucille in a small brasserie in the Boulevard de Clichy. Lucille had been animated on the subject of the express murder.

'I think she might know something,' his man told Mettefeu. 'Shall I bring her in?'

'Without delay,' Mettefeu ordered.

In Mettefeu's office the young woman was considerably less animated than in the Clichy bar.

'What's this all about?' she demanded, but she was plainly putting on a front. Under it she was apprehensive, and trying to keep the fact a secret. Mettefeu gave her no chance to recover her shaken nerve.

'What do you know about the Riviera Express murder?' he asked.

'Nothing, except – ' She hesitated, but plunged, feeling she had no alternative under Mettefeu's sharp eye. She told him her good looks had won the admiring glances of a man who was a conductor on a Paris bus line. His name was Guerrier, and according to Lucille he liked having a good time, which meant attending dance-halls and restaurants where there was plenty of noise and lights. Lucille liked him because he was good company. Soon after, Guerrier had introduced her to another man, who was a stranger to her. As she put it, he was dressed to knock one's eye out.

'He obviously thought a lot of himself,' she said.

'Describe him,' Mettefeu told her. Mettefeu heard again of the sharp dresser with the pale gloves. He also heard that this man had boasted of being on what he had termed 'the express job'.

'You believed him?' Mettefeu asked.

The woman sneered. 'Just a lie to impress me. But if one could believe him the police are in for a thin time, monsieur.' She added impressively, 'According to Guerrier's pal it won't be guns next time, but bombs.'

If there was any truth in the woman's assertion it meant this man who wore pale gloves and dressed in extravagantly cut clothes was an anarchist. They were the killers who preferred bombs for their greater power of destruction than bullets. The possibility that bombs might be thrown soon stimulated Mettefeu to speedy action. He told his men to bring in Guerrier, who told

Mettefeu when questioned that this man was someone he knew as André. He knew little about the man. He was a café acquaintance, that was all. He agreed that André liked boasting. But Guerrier had an item of news that registered with the Brigade chief. A short while before the Riviera Express was held up André had hinted that something would soon happen that would make the front pages. He had shown Guerrier a velvet mask and a ticket to Nice.

When Guerrier had begun questioning him he had grinned and said, 'Don't ask.'

Guerrier was shown the velvet scraps from Nolay. He agreed that they seemed to be of the same material and colour as the mask André had shown him.

'If you want to reach this André,' the Brigade chief asked, 'where would you go?'

Guerrier wasn't happy about giving an answer, but one was expected of him and it had to be the truth. He said hesitantly, 'The Brasserie de la Paix in the Rue Cujas', and received an unpleasant surprise.

Mettefeu told him, 'We'll rig you up and tonight you'll come with us.'

The disguised bus conductor and four Special Brigade detectives kept watch on the brasserie that evening, but André did not appear. After waiting some hours Mettefeu went inside and questioned the proprietor, who shook his head and said he didn't know this André. Mettefeu questioned the waiters. One said he recognized the description given by Mettefeu. He said the man had been in earlier and had phoned a friend at the Hôtel Excelsior, which was lower down the Rue Cujas. Mettefeu went to the hotel, where he found that a message phoned for Monsieur Brégère was remembered, but unfortunately Marcel Brégère had left two days before. His departure had been quite sudden because he had booked his room for a month.

'Do you know where he's gone?' Mettefeu inquired.

'No, monsieur,' said the hotel manager, 'but he hasn't cancelled his room.'

'What does that mean?'

'He left instructions,' Mettefeu was told, 'that it was to be retained for a Mademoiselle Vialle. At the moment she is in hospital, but is expected out shortly. So we're holding the room for her.'

'Who is she?' Mettefeu asked.

'A friend of Monsieur Brégère's.' The hotel manager shrugged as though that should be explanation enough.

Mettefeu tried to get the man to tell him something about André, who had phoned Marcel Brégère, but the manager kept shaking his head until Mettefeu mentioned the pale gloves. He looked interested and said André could be Monsieur Cablane, someone who had once stayed for a week at the hotel and who had been friendly with Marcel Brégère who was a sculptor. He checked that the man had been absent from his hotel room on the night of the murder. On the following day he had returned with his clothes noticeably creased and rumpled, and he had appeared both tired and irritable.

'Show me this room he has left for Mademoiselle Vialle,' Mettefeu instructed the manager.

He was taken upstairs to the room, which was unlocked for him. He searched thoroughly, but found nothing save a fragment of a letter which was under a carpet. He made out the sprawled handwriting as:

'Go to the Hôtel de Grenoble and find if Dujardin has returned from Rouen.'

Mettefeu pocketed this find and returned downstairs to ask for the hotel register. He found no record of Cablane staying there, and next questioned the staff, one of whom admitted that a Monsieur Charrier, a medical student who had stayed in the hotel about three years earlier, was very similar in build and appearance to Cablane.

Returning to his office, Mettefeu sent a man to make a check with the files of the Service des Garnis, which records the names of hotel guests. The man came back to report that there was an Hôtel de Grenoble in the same *arrondissement* or ward of the city, but neither Charrier nor Cablane appeared in its listed returns of hotel guests, although a Gaston Dujardin had booked in on the day following that when Cablane was said to have left the Excelsior. Like most hard-bitten detectives of experience, Mettefeu was not an easy man to convince with a coincidence.

To him what he had just been told amounted to more than coincidence. He had his team go through the files of known criminals again. They found neither Cablane nor Dujardin, but a Charrier had seen the inside of prison. His photograph was procured and taken to the Excelsior and shown to the members of the staff. Two of them said they were convinced Cablane was Charrier.

This painstaking process was repeated at the Grenoble, where Charrier was readily recognized. But not as Cablane. As Dujardin! As though his persistence deserved a reward, Mettefeu was told the man himself had entered only a matter of minutes before. He was wearing pale gloves and carrying a walking-stick. Mettefeu began to feel he was making progress of a real kind now. But he had no mind to rush things. He considered it wiser to wait until Brégère contacted the man at the Grenoble. Watch was kept on the hotel throughout the night. Brégère did not arrive, but when the man with pale gloves left the hotel he was arrested. In his pocket Mettefeu found an automatic with a full clip of cartridges.

The dandified crook appeared stunned by his arrest, and was not hesitant in telling Mettefeu he had two accomplices, Bertrand and Thomas. Brégère was Bertrand.

'I've been expecting a visit from him,' the arrested man complained.

'All in good time,' Mettefeu promised. 'You'll see each other again.'

Charrier seemed anxious to please the police now he was in custody, as though placating them might ameliorate his plight. Shown files of photographs, he picked out his associates and explained where they usually went for food or a drink. When he had committed himself this far Mettefeu suddenly changed tactics and became the unrelenting cop. He demanded how the Riviera Express hold-up had been planned.

Charrier explained that the three crooks had met in prison. After being released they had teamed up. Their first job was a flat in Marseilles. From that they went on to bigger and more ambitious crimes. Then they had come to Paris and that was where the 'big one', as Charrier called it, was planned. The final arrangements were made on Friday, 23 July. The next

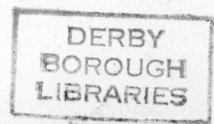

night the Riviera Express would provide good pickings and plenty. Their plan, after buying through tickets to Nice, was to rob the passengers and then leave the train at Dijon, the capital of Burgundy. Lieutenant Carabelli's brave resistance had demanded an abrupt change of plans.

According to Charrier the ringleader was Thomas.

Mettefeu made sure there was no leak to the reporters who were camped at police headquarters while a thorough search was made for the wanted pair. They were finally reported sitting at a table outside a café in the Place des Ternes. Two Brigade members took a table close by. More of Mettefeu's men arrived and took up positions down the street.

The men under observation were plainly jittery. Something must have alarmed them. They rose, and after throwing some money on the table started to cross the road. Mettefeu's men moved to close in on them. The crooks realized what was happening and drew automatics. The next moment the Place des Ternes echoed to gunfire, which was returned by the armed police.

Thomas dropped dead. Bertrand fell wounded, still firing, and four of his bullets ripped into Inspector Curnier. The detective and the man who had killed him died almost at the same moment.

Mecislas Charrier, the bastard son of a Russian, was the only member of the bandit gang to stand trial. By that time he had fully recovered his shattered nerve. He defied the jury to 'take his head'. The jury took him up on it, and he was guillotined on 22 August 1922.

Before that memorable Paris trial took place the dead inspector, who had posthumously been awarded the Legion of Honour, was buried on a day when it seemed all Paris had turned out to pay homage to a gallant detective who was sincerely mourned.

6 THE CHAIN OF
CIRCUMSTANCE

About seven years after Brigadier Mettefeu in Paris had kept a promise made to the anarchist Mecislas Charrier by showing him the bodies of his dead companions in crime a man named Messiter disappeared in Southampton.

He had been the manager of an oil company, a man who lived, so far as his employers, the Wolfe's Head Oil Company, knew, without any pressing personal problems, and his work had been satisfactory and consistent. But, for no known reason, Messiter had decided to leave his employment and the day he made that decision apparently was 30 October 1928.

That was the day he locked the door of the garage premises in Southampton where he had his office and vanished. After waiting a couple of months the oil company appointed a new representative to take over the missing Messiter's post in Southampton.

The new man had been told that Messiter's landlord in the town had gone to the police a week after the disappearance and it was suggested that he might make a few tactful inquiries on his own.

Accordingly on the evening of 9 January 1929, the new manager for the Wolfe's Head Oil Company paid a visit to the home of a Mr Parrot in Carlton Road, Southampton. He had a legitimate reason for making the call. Parrot had been Vivian Messiter's landlord, for the oil company's missing manager had lodged with the Parrot family, and the man who had taken Messiter's place wanted to find out if the key of the Southampton depot, which was also missing, had been left in Messiter's lodgings.

He did not come by the key as a result of his call, but the man who opened the door to him told him the facts of what seemed to be a curious mystery.

Vivian Messiter's clothing still hung in the wardrobe in the room that had been his. His shaving tackle was still where Mrs Parrot had put it, and his underclothes remained in the drawers of a chest. For more than two months the Parrots had been waiting word from the missing man, but he had not written or wired them what to do with his personal effects.

' I left it a week and then I went to the police,' Parrot told the Wolfe's Head man.

He related how he had accompanied a police officer to the Wolfe's Head depot in Grove Street, which Parrot's lodger had been in the habit of referring to as the garage. They had found the main gates enclosing building and yard locked. The yard beyond had looked deserted. Next door was a public house, separated from the Wolfe's Head premises by a wall, over which Parrot and the policeman climbed. They crossed the yard to be confronted by the warehouse door, which was secured with a stout padlock.

The policeman broke a pane of glass in a window, lit a candle he had brought, and held the tiny flame inside the building at arm's length. The thin light flickered over the shadowy shapes of bins and drums of oil and the peering men outside made out the shape of a car. The place looked as though no one had been there for a considerable time.

' Nothing else we can do, the place is empty,' said the policeman.

He led the way back over the wall. When he had made out his report some inquiries were made among Messiter's acquaintances. None of them could offer a reason for his disappearance.

After hearing the story told by Parrot the new manager asked if he could see the room Messiter had rented. He was shown the way upstairs. He stood in the middle of the room staring round.

' I really came hoping the key of the padlock would be here,' he admitted.

Mrs Parrot told him she had cleaned the room thoroughly several times and had not found any keys.

'At least he took his keys with him,' she said. 'Like his money. We've still got rent owing.'

The following morning the new manager broke into his firm's premises. It was a gloomy warehouse, cold and airless, with too little light and too many draughts. There was an untidy sprawl of packing cases. Some were empty, some partly empty, some full of cans of oil. His job would be to arrange for selling the oil. The stone floor was littered with rat dungs and filth and dried oil stains.

The new manager walked around his domain, feeling critical of the state of the place and of Vivian Messiter who had left it like this. He crossed to the dusty car. Packing cases were stacked in tiers behind it, with narrow passages between the stacks. It was the darkest part of the warehouse. He pushed his way between two of the mounds of packing cases and came to an abrupt halt. The whereabouts of Vivian Messiter were no longer a mystery. The man had not left the premises of the Wolfe's Head Oil Company. The new manager instinctively started to bend over the body he had found, then straightened, flinching. A bad smell was coming up in the dark chill of that January morning. The rats had already feasted on the head and there were dark stains on the stone flags.

The new manager squeezed round between the piled cases of oil and crossed back to the lighter part of the warehouse. He felt sick and rather faint and he had to clench his teeth to prevent them from chattering.

Later that day a police surgeon had some difficulty in coming to a conclusion about the dead man. The grim state of the ravaged head made it difficult for him to decide whether Vivian Messiter had been shot through the head or brutally clubbed to death. About the only thing he was sure of was that the dead man had been murdered.

However, the murderer had emptied the victim's pockets of any money they had contained. He had left some letters, but they seemed of scant value in a murder inquiry. On the floor of the garage a glove was found. Lying under it was a signet ring which had presumably been torn from the dead man's hand but had rolled away in the darkness and been concealed by the glove.

In total, it was very little, as the Chief Constable of South-ampton, Mr McCormac, realized when the few known details were passed to him. He acted without delay in summoning help from Scotland Yard, and the two detectives of the CID sent to assist the Southampton Police were Chief Inspector John Prothero and Sergeant Hugh Young.

The Yard men almost did not get to Southampton, for earlier that morning they had been sent in a different direction out of London on what had turned out to be a wild-goose chase. A woman had reported that a man had been murdered and his body buried in the same grave as a horse. The woman had even sworn an affidavit before a Commissioner of Oaths to this effect. But Prothero and Young, who were a regular team of Yard detectives, soon proved the claim held no truth. As Hugh Young said many years later, after retiring from forty years at Scotland Yard with the rank of Commander (Crime), CID, 'Inquiry showed that she had a grudge against the world in general and her near neighbour in particular, and eventually she admitted that the whole thing was a complete fabrication.'

That little exercise on 10 January 1929 was in the nature of a warm-up for what was to come later the same day, when the Yard's Chief Constable Fred Wensley broke the news of the Southampton murder and told them to lose no time getting there. They were in time to repack their bags and catch the ten-thirty evening train from Waterloo, which arrived in Southamp-ton half an hour after midnight.

They were hurried to Bargate police station, where arrange-ments had been made for putting them up, and after a short night's rest they joined Inspector Chatfield, who was able to tell them as much as the local police knew, which was disappoint-ingly little.

The two most promising clues already discovered in a search of the storeroom were a couple of books. One was a cheap exer-cise book, the other a book of duplicate invoices containing a couple of much-used sheets of carbon paper.

Prothero accompanied the police surgeon to the mortuary and although he had been prepared he still received a shock when he was shown the remains of Vivian Messiter, a man who was known to have come from a good family, of ancient Somerset stock. The Yard detective could not afford to be squeamish. With the police surgeon he examined the appalling head and came to the decision Messiter had not been shot, but bludgeoned to death.

When later Sir Bernard Spilsbury, the well-known Home Office pathologist, made his own examination of the remains he agreed with Prothero's assessment.

The dead man's clothes were examined, but they provided nothing unusual, and the Yard detectives called at 3 Carlton Road to interview the Parrots, who once more repeated their story and showed the way to the room that had been the dead man's.

Once more Prothero found nothing to help him.

Messiter had not been a very orderly man in his ways. He had kept few records and undertaken little correspondence. Also, he had made no regular note of phone calls.

However, Prothero did find among the dead man's things a letter from a W. F. Thomas, who apparently was unemployed and seeking a post as travelling salesman on commission. Thomas's address was given as 5 Cranbery Avenue, Southampton, and the way the letter was couched suggested that the writer was replying to an advertisement Messiter had inserted in a local paper.

It seemed to be the result of an ordinary day-to-day transaction. The letter was placed in a file Prothero began to collect.

A fresh search of the unsavoury warehouse was organized and the car was removed for closer examination. The two books had been found on one of its seats. The piles of packing cases were dismantled and examined. The floor was swept and the piles of filth removed. It became possible to breathe reasonably fresh cold air in the place. This tidying-up operation produced a reward for Prothero in the form of a small gold ring, still fairly bright, so that it could not have been lying where it was found for more than some two months. At some time it had received a severe wrench. This had opened it. Prothero thought the ring might have come from a watch-chain that had been tugged, possibly in a struggle.

He had been told by the Parrots that Vivian Messiter had

normally worn a watch and chain, but such an article had not been found on the corpse or in Messiter's room.

Something else produced by the cleaning process was a scrap of torn and crumpled paper. It was first seen covered with sawdust. When Prothero smoothed it out he found part of a written receipt:

> 5 Cranbery Ave
> Oct. 20th
> With thanks
>> Horne

On the reverse was some writing in indelible pencil that was indecipherable through the grease stain and dirt on the paper.

In the small room at the rear of the warehouse that had been used as an office Prothero found another piece of screwed-up paper. It looked as though it had been crumpled in a hand and tossed away.

When he opened it out he had a sheet of notepaper bearing the letterhead of the Wolfe's Head Oil Company. The sheet had writing on both sides. On one, written in pencil, he read:

> Mr W. F. Thomas,
>> I shall be at 42 Grove Street at ten,
> but not at noon.
>> Vivian Messiter

The scrawled signature was recognizable. On the reverse was the name 'Mr W. F. Thomas.' It was in the same handwriting. It seemed that Messiter had written this note but not posted it because it was to be collected. The issue for Prothero was whether Thomas had received it, had called at the Grove Street premises, and had then thrown away the crumpled note in the office.

It was after finding the note in the office that he found the murder weapon. It was a large heavy hammer, rather similar to the one Capstick found later at Cadno Farm buried by its handle. The iron head was smeared with dried blood that had turned black. From this paint-like substance protruded some shortish dark hairs. Later they were found to match the hair of Messiter's eyebrows.

That was the sum of John Prothero's findings.

As was to be expected, the murder was by this time receiving a good deal of attention in the newspapers. So Prothero knew that the killer was not ignorant of the fact that his crime was being investigated. What the Yard man was careful to ensure was that no word of his finds appeared in any of the newspaper stories. In the Yard chief inspector's opinion the murderer had done a hurried job, like a man in a panic. He should have taken time to remove the watch and chain instead of tugging it from his victim's waistcoat so that the small gold linkring was widened and lost. He should have taken away the weapon he had used. He should also have been more careful about the pieces of paper. Perhaps hands that were so agitated that they fumbled and dropped a signet ring would have fumbled with matches had he tried to burn the scraps of paper.

Prothero realized that he was now approaching the establishment of a possible motive. The evidence of the hammer pointed to Messiter being struck in the face while facing his killer. At least, in this case, there was a suggestion of a heated argument ending in a quarrel and the killer snatching up the first weapon to hand. In this case the crime would be unpremeditated. The signs of haste afterwards supported this. As a theory, all this amounted to was the possibility that the unknown killer was an impetuous person of violent instincts. Was W. F. Thomas such a person?

However, when Prothero and Young found that Thomas had left his lodging at 5 Cranbery Avenue they felt there was reason to consider with suspicion the man who had answered an advertisement. At this stage a telephone call from someone named Mitchell who lived in Downton, a village not far from Southampton, offered direction for extending their search. The caller had read the newspaper accounts of the garage murder and had been intrigued by the name Thomas. He said he had good reason to remember a man of that name, who had swindled him. According to the angry caller, this person calling himself Thomas had arrived in the village a few days after Vivian Messiter had been murdered, towards the end of the previous October. He had been looking for work, he claimed, and Mitchell had taken him on. After a few days Thomas had left without saying goodbye. With him had gone £143 of Mitchell's money.

It could conceivably be the same Thomas, but checking would take more time than the two Yard men could devote to it. The Southampton Police were asked to handle this part of the investigation. Prothero concentrated on Cranbery Avenue, where he learned that Thomas had arrived with his wife on 20 October. The landlady was a Mrs Horne, to whom he had paid ten shillings deposit on the room.

'I gave him a receipt,' she told Prothero, who took a piece of paper from his pocket and offered it to her.

'Is this it?'

'Part of it. It's been torn.'

This confirmation meant that both pieces of paper found at the garage referred to W. F. Thomas.

Prothero went to the offices of the *Southern Daily Echo*. He had Vivian Messiter's advertisement found, and also another that had been inserted by Mr Mitchell of Downton, who had wanted a competent motor mechanic. He was able to check through the newspaper's files that Thomas had replied to the advertisements on 22 October. The next day, the 23rd, Messiter had called on Thomas at Cranbery Avenue. When he left Thomas accompanied him in Messiter's car, which Mrs Horne identified as the one left in the garage.

Mitchell had also contacted Thomas and arranged to meet him at Bar Gate, in Southampton, on the 26th. Thomas had promised to come out to Downton in a few days.

This was proof that the two men named Thomas were the same person and Prothero did not have to rely on vague personal descriptions. Moreover, the jobs made a pattern. Messiter had given him a job on commission as a salesman, and Mitchell a job in a repair garage at a weekly wage. He had started at once with Messiter, and Prothero was able to prove that he had been seen travelling in Messiter's car to several addresses in Southampton. He had taken up his job with Mitchell on 5 November.

Two days before that he and the woman he claimed was his wife left Cranbery Avenue. But no Mrs Thomas had arrived with him in Downton. To Prothero this suggested that the woman had gone off on her own. Most likely she was not his wife and had refused to stay with Thomas when she knew of what had happened at the garage.

Whoever he was, Thomas was a stubborn villain and had a cool nerve, for he had not run when he had left Mitchell's garage at the time the money disappeared. The local police had found him still living in the village and had questioned him. He had denied taking the money and claimed that earlier he had been employed by the Allied Road Transport Association, which had offices in Bold Street, Southampton. Because they did not find the money or anyone who had seen Thomas with it, the police could not bring a charge against him and his former employer was left feeling angry and cheated, which was his reason for phoning the police again after reading about the body found in the Grove Street warehouse. In the meantime Thomas, affecting injured pride, had left Downton.

It was inevitable, with the case proliferating in this way, that Prothero and Young should find themselves wasting time in running down false leads. But because they worked long hours and slept few they were successful in locating a lorry driver who, on the day Thomas disappeared from Downton, gave a lift to a man answering Thomas's description. He was accompanied by a woman who answered Mrs Horne's description of Mrs Thomas. He had taken the couple as far as Salisbury. There in the city intensive checking satisfied Prothero that the woman had been left in Salisbury while Thomas doubled back in his tracks. He had taken a taxi to Downton and told the driver to go through the village and pull up on the far side. When Prothero spoke to the taxi driver the man recalled looking in his mirror, just before stopping, and seeing Thomas down on the floor. When the taxi turned and stopped Thomas got out.

'Won't keep you long,' he said before making off across the fields that were misty. He came back after a few minutes, dishevelled and out of breath. 'All right, driver, back to Salisbury,' he had ordered. To Prothero it seemed possible that Thomas had come back to recover the stolen money from where it had been concealed, and he had not brought the woman because he had not trusted her fully. Additional inquiries by a network of plain-clothes men produced evidence that the pair had later hired a car to take them to London.

Prothero collected from the Hampshire police the only thing in the nature of a clue they had found in Thomas's room at Downton. This was a slip of pink paper bearing the name of a garage in Manchester. Prothero had inquiries made there, and the firm replied that the description of the man Prothero was interested in fitted someone known to them as William Henry Podmore, who had been employed by them on 17 October and soon afterwards had absconded with one of the firm's cars.

Now a nationwide search for Podmore and the woman was begun by police throughout the country. Clues obtained in London pointed to his having made for Birmingham, the blonde woman who had been Mrs Thomas still with him. As a matter of fact, this quarry Prothero was hunting had secured a job in a hotel at Meriden, six miles outside Coventry. But when his photo appeared in the national newspapers he left without collecting the wages due to him. Podmore and the blonde were on the run. They doubled back to Birmingham, made for the Potteries, where the woman had relatives, but after only a brief stay the pair were back in Birmingham.

The close police follow-up, although always some steps behind a couple who were now fugitives receiving a good deal of Press publicity, produced some interesting enlargement on the woman. In certain Midlands underworld circles she was known as Golden-haired Lil. This was the human-interest angle featured in a great many Press reports. All Britain knew that the police were looking for a man with a small scar on one side of his face, and that the wanted man was accompanied by a woman with bright blonde hair.

Indeed, it was not only the closeness of the police pursuit, but the space devoted to the wanted pair by the newspapers, that decided Podmore and the woman to separate. Lil of the golden hair returned to her relatives in the Potteries. Podmore, back to using his own name, though for how long no policeman in England could rightly guess, caught a train for London, bent on hiding in the Big Smoke. It was a desperate move rather than a clever one, for he had not been installed long in a small hotel in the Vauxhall Bridge Road when he was reported by the Flying Squad. Within hours he was picked up. He told the police with brazen effrontery that he was lying low and gave them a reason.

'I'm keeping out of sight after the Stone job,' he said.

This was the purest bluff. He was referring to a burglary of some time before in Staffordshire. Jewellery had been taken by Podmore who was then using the name of Stone. Interviewed by the local police his glib tongue had won him release, as it had at Downton. The stolen jewels were missing and suspicion wasn't enough. But it enabled Podmore to use one crime to put up an alibi about a worse one – murder.

He was taken to Southampton. It was Hugh Young's job to take down in longhand the questions put to Podmore and the answers he provided. In answering Podmore made a bad error. When asked how he had met Messiter, he said through an agent named Baxton or Maxton. This agent and Messister had a book in which they made entries. Of what, he claimed he did not know, but money had passed between them. Having said this much he stopped and, looking suddenly uncertain, asked Young, 'What have you put down?'

When the sergeant read out his rambling answer Podmore lost his temper.

'That's not what I said,' he shouted. After some moments he calmed down and said, 'Messiter made that entry, not this Maxton fellow or whatever his name is.'

To Prothero this point seemed to hold some secret significance. When he returned to London he again examined the old exercise book, which seemed to be the book Podmore had referred to, and he came upon the following entry :

Oct. 30th/28

Received from
Wolfe Head Oil Co.
Commission on order
S. Gover –
5 galls. heavy at 6d. – 2/6

Beside the '2/6' was written in a sloping hand 'H. F. Galton.' The writing of the entry was in Messiter's more upright hand. Only the signature was in Galton's writing. Was this Galton the Baxton or Maxton of Podmore's statement?

One of the letters left in the dead man's pockets was from

A. (or H.) F. Galton of 163 Oakley Road, Shirley, Southampton. Mr Galton was a railway employee who had agreed to do spare-time travelling for Wolfe's Head. Prothero found that he had obtained only one order for Messiter's firm. This had been given him by Mr S. Gover, whose name appeared in the exercise book. Messiter had delivered the oil at the agent's address the day before his murder, 29 October. The commission of sixpence per gallon had been paid, but Messiter had made an ironic error in the date. He had put the next day, the date of his own murder, by mistake.

Mr Galton's daughter was certain the date was the 29th, and her father said he had not visited the Grove Street depot.

Prothero gave the exercise book a closer scrutiny and found that a page had been torn from it. The missing page had preceded the one recording Galton's commission for the Gover sale.

Many years later Hugh Young recorded the next important moments of the case when he wrote :

Suddenly, as Prothero held the book up to the light, a ray striking the paper slantwise seemed to throw up in relief the shadowy outline of some writing on the page on which our eyes were focused. It was not actual writing, but only the very faint impression left on the page underneath the one which had been torn out, and on which the actual message had been written.

To the naked eye the impressions were not legible, and they only became a shade more visible by holding the book so that the light fell obliquely across the page. It was a moment of tense excitement. 'We must get it photographed,' said Prothero. So James O'Brien, one of the Yard's experts in photography, took a preliminary photograph there and then, by oblique light from a 2,000-candle-power arc-lamp.

The following was found to be the impression :

Oct 28/28

Received from
    Wolfe Head Oil Co.
    Commission on Cromers and Bartlett –
        5 galls. at 6d. – 2/6

Beside this '2/6' were the initials 'W.F.T.'

Obviously Thomas had come across the Galton receipt when he was ripping out the page containing his own, and must have realized the significance and importance to him of that wrong date. This was his reason for leaving the book on the seat of the car, where it was sure to be found when the garage was searched.

The exercise book was sent to Dr Ainsworth Mitchell and Bernard Ellis, handwriting experts who had been shown the scraps of paper. They too photographed the impressions in the exercise book, compared the formation of the words with Thomas's writing, and declared Thomas had written the missing page from which the impressions were received. They had deciphered the torn receipt found at the garage as follows:

> Possibly 36 Galls. Tuesday
> 12 Galls. beginning of week
> W. F. Thomas
> Call at gar – Sat – 10 am or 12.0

The writing was Podmore's, which made the crumpled note found in the garage office and signed by Messiter the answer to this note.

The invoice book was examined microscopically, but it was an address recorded on one of the carbon sheets that held Prothero's interest – Cromers and Bartlett, Bold Street, Southampton. Bold Street was the address Thomas had given the Hampshire police for the fictitious Allied Road Transport Association when questioned in Downton.

'Bold Street' was a similar piece of fiction. This could mean only one thing. The order was a fake and Messiter had been tricked into paying commission on dummy orders. The carbon sheets were photographed and the negatives rephotographed to reverse the effect and these prints were again photographed, this time with enlarging lenses, and the new prints treated with specially coloured inks. Fresh addresses were picked out from the maze of criss-cross lines. All were checked and all were found to be non-existent!

The killer's motive was at last clear. He had murdered Messiter when the swindle became known to the Wolfe's Head man. But the list of fake addresses was sent to the Staffordshire police, because Podmore, like his Golden-haired Lil, came from the

Stoke-upon-Trent area, and Prothero had an idea a man providing false addresses in the South might use Potteries names as being unfamiliar. This check proved very rewarding – and surprising. As in the choice of the name Baskeyfield – the name of a police sergeant who had once arrested Podmore in his home area! Even Cromer and Bartlett was a name of a Potteries firm, but they proved they had never given an order to the Wolfe's Head company. 'Bold Street', too, was a giveaway. There were three streets of that name around Stoke.

Podmore was arrested, but justice was prepared to take its time. He was charged with the theft of a car in Manchester, convicted, and sent to Strangeways for six months. In the Northern prison he boasted to a fellow prisoner of how he had robbed his employer in Downton of £143. When he was released from Strangeways he was arrested on this charge and taken to London for trial at the Old Bailey, where he was again convicted and went to Wandsworth Prison for six months. He still could not resist talking to fellow prisoners, and he convinced a couple that he had indeed murdered Vivian Messiter. On 17 December he had about a quarter of an hour of freedom when he was again released, for as he stepped outside the prison's tall gates it was to be confronted by Prothero, his personal man of doom, who was holding a fresh warrant for his arrest. This time on a murder charge. If ever a prisoner learned the hard way that crime doesn't pay he was William Podmore.

He still was under thirty when he was tried at Winchester Assizes for Messiter's murder, with Lord Hewart, the Lord Chief Justice, presiding, who made one thing very clear to the jury when he told them, ' Circumstantial evidence consists in this, that when you look at all the surrounding circumstances you find such a series of undesigned, unexpected coincidences that as a reasonable person you find your judgement is compelled to one conclusion.' The unbreakable chain of circumstances forged by Prothero and Young in a truly memorable piece of investigation left that jury of one mind. They expressed it when they brought in their verdict of ' Guilty'.

Podmore had his eyes closed as Lord Hewart sentenced him to death. Just possibly he was revising an opinion expressed to another prisoner in Wandsworth.

Podmore had told the man, 'The old farmers in Hampshire don't know how to try a man.'

Too late he was learning how many errors he had made in a short but continuous and vicious life of crime.

7 MURDER WHILE
THE CHOIR SANG

When Inspector Ruyter of Amsterdam and some of his colleagues of the Dutch Criminal Police took a man to church it was possibly for the most bizarre gathering in the history of St Peter's, Bylderdyk. They were not about to attend a service, nor to inspect the building in an appreciative mood. They were there to re-enact a murder.

In more formal terms they were about to reconstruct a crime for the police record before a man charged with murder was brought to trial.

The crime had been committed some time before and the victim was a stonemason named Kobus Polder, a married man whose conscientious application to his craft had seemingly earned him recognition from his employer. He had been taken into partnership because his work was indispensable to the firm.

When it was found, following an architectural survey, that the church tower of St Peter's required substantial repairs Polder's firm was asked to undertake the work on condition that it was completed before Christmas, so that the scaffolding would be cleared away before midnight Mass on Christmas Eve. Polder went to the church, and estimated how long the task would take.

'I will work on the tower myself,' he told the church officials. 'It will be ready by Christmas.'

He began the work in the autumn, and for weeks he was a lonely figure perched high on his web of scaffolding, like some industrious spider, as he hacked away at stone that had been made porous and weak by the bitter salt winds from the North Sea. He came to measure his week by events that happened in the church, the mid-week services, the weddings and funerals, the meetings for choir practice and organ music. He told his wife, 'One can't help feeling a little nearer to the angels working up there between earth and heaven.' This piece of artisan's whimsy held considerably more truth than he realized.

The next time he was on his scaffold repairing the tower and listening to the voices of the choir and the resonant chords arising from the organ he was a man close to death. It was early evening and he was working to complete the removal of a particularly bad piece of rotted stonework before he left to go home to the evening meal his wife would have waiting for him. They had no children, and when he was late she fretted. With the nights drawing in he did not wish to leave her alone too long.

In the church below the organist played some chords which died away as a soloist's voice rose clear and flutelike. From outside something clattered noisily. This sound was followed by a spilled cry of alarm and fear, which was broken off abruptly and followed almost immediately by another sound. Something bulky had hit the scaffolding with a dull impact.

The soloist stopped on a high note. The organist finished on a note that was a protest. The choir looked at one another, alarmed and fearful. On a shared impulse they moved from their places in the choir stalls and made their way to the side door leading outside at the base of the tower. In a soft gloom they stood peering at a human form sprawled in an unnatural posture across part of the scaffolding, some twenty feet over their heads.

Below the scaffolding lay an overturned bucket, scattered pieces of stone debris, and the stonemason's hammer.

'We must tell the police,' the choirmaster decided. 'Also the fire brigade, because they will be needed to get him down.'

It was thought Polder might have had a stroke. But the police surgeon who examined the body after the fireman had lowered it into a carpet from the church decided that death resulted from a blow to the scalp as though made with a heavy instrument. In falling the dead man had broken several ribs and crushed his pelvis against the scaffolding.

The police soon made sure that Polder had been alone when he fell, for his partner and former employer, Jacob van Peit, said that he and another workman, a carpenter, had left for the night half an hour before what he called the terrible accident.

The police remained disturbed by the nature of the dead man's scalp wound. They sent a report to the Public Prosecutor, but had to state that they had discovered no evidence of the death being due to anything other than an accident. It looked as though the death of Kobus Polder was just another statistic in the official records when the burial certificate was issued. His widow faced a bleak Christmas.

More than a year later police in Haarlem, which is a few miles west of Amsterdam and not far from the Dutch coast, saw a light flickering in a villa late one night and surprised a burglar. His name was Wilhelm Petersen, and the local police believed they had caught a man responsible for a series of burglaries in the past weeks.

Petersen was in no position to plead innocence, and his finger-prints were taken as a matter of routine. However, the Haarlem police were shaken when a check with criminal records showed that the captured man's fingerprints were not at police head-quarters. Yet they were convinced that the series of local burglaries had been carried out by a professional thief. Could it be that they had at last caught up with a successful crook who so far had evaded capture?

They checked Petersen's background, found that he had been born at The Hague in 1910 and had been apprenticed as a young man to a shipwright. However, meagre pay and long hours had not appealed to him, and he had gone to sea as a ship's car-penter. After five years roving the oceans of the world he had returned to shore life. First as a carpenter in Groningen, in north-east Holland, then in Brussels before returning to Holland and working in Rotterdam, another port.

Petersen maintained that his breaking into the villa at Haarlem was his first attempt at burglary, and in support of this told the police he had recently been working for Jacob van Peit, who had a builders' firm in Amsterdam.

' Why did you leave?'

' Because of an injury to my back.'

He was asked how the injury had occurred and where, ques-tions which made it plain that the police would check his answers.

'While I was working on a repair job to a church,' he told them. 'St Peter's, Bylderdyk.'

Petersen's story was related in a report that duly appeared on the desk of Inspector Ruyter in Amsterdam. The inspector wasn't satisfied with Petersen's account of how he had taken to crime. The captured man had said he had been helped for a time with sums of money from Jacob van Peit, but after his former employer had left Amsterdam the payments had stopped. He questioned Petersen.

'This injury meant you couldn't climb a scaffold or ladder any more?'

'That's right,' said Petersen. 'It hurt my back too much.'

'Yet you could climb through a window into a house. How was that?'

Petersen was silent. Ruyter asked him where he had received treatment for his injured back and was told the other had no faith in doctors and he didn't trust hospitals.

'So you didn't have anyone examine your injured back?'

'No,' Petersen admitted.

When asked where Jacob van Peit had gone he said he didn't know, but later he told Inspector Ruyter that a Mrs Polder living in Overtoom might be able to give him van Peit's address.

Ruyter discovered that Mrs Polder was the widow of a man who had died tragically a little more than a year before while working on the same church where Petersen claimed to have injured his back. He also learned that after the death of her husband Mrs Polder had rented rooms to her husband's partner.

He called on her, and found her to be obviously annoyed at the mention of both men, van Peit and Petersen. She said she didn't know the present whereabouts of the former, for whom she appeared to have little liking, but she was openly hostile in her attitude towards the burglar.

'That man's no good and I have no wish to discuss him,' she said and proved it by refusing to say anything more about Petersen.

Ruyter left feeling distinctly baffled. He also felt that in some way he had been challenged and decided doggedly to find van Peit. He had his men make inquiries of merchants who might have supplied van Peit with materials and tools and the general

equipment of a builder usually engaged in repair and maintenance work. They came back and told him the general feeling in
the trade was that van Peit had skipped after running up a good
many debts. A few of the men to whom he owed money thought
he might set up again in another town. One had mentioned The
Hague as a possibility.

Ruyter went to the Dutch capital and had fresh inquiries made
there. Within a few hours he knew where Jacob van Peit had
opened a fresh business. He called the next day, and found the
builder to be a big-framed man with an oily voice and sharp
eyes, who gave no hint of being embarrassed by the visit of a
detective from Amsterdam. When told Ruyter wanted some
facts about his employment of a man named Wilhelm Petersen
he smiled.

'Now there was a man I liked,' he said gushingly. 'Wish I
could find him now. He was a good worker and I was sorry I
had to let him go because things got so slack. I had to move out
myself.'

Ruyter inquired if the other man recalled Petersen injuring
his back. Van Peit's reaction suggested that he found the question an awkward one to answer simply and directly. Instead, he
began a rambling recital about occupational hazards in building
work, and after he had gained time to consider a reply he confided that he couldn't recall Petersen having an accident that
could be described as serious. Someone was lying – or possibly
more than one.

Ruyter informed the builder that Petersen had claimed to
have hurt his back so badly that he could not continue at his
employment. At this van Peit's round face clouded. He put on
an expression suggesting he was taxing his memory to recall
something that had happened not very long before. The act was
not very convincing to Ruyter. At last the builder gave an ex-
clamation of surprise and said he had just remembered something. He had just recalled Petersen having an accident during
the repair work on St Peter's, the same unfortunate job on
which his partner had fallen to his death. Then van Peit became
curious in his turn.

'You're very interested in Petersen, inspector,' he pointed out.
'What's he done?'

' We're holding him on a charge of burglary, mynheer,' Ruyter said bluntly.

' Not Petersen!' van Peit exclaimed.

' You said he was a good man. Is that right?'

' Absolutely. Like I said, if he turned up now I'd give him a job right away.'

Ruyter now had the feeling that, in some way, both men were covering for each other, Petersen for van Peit and van Peit for Petersen. But why? When he left the Hague to return to Amsterdam he had a growing feeling that the pair were involved with each other in some deal both wanted to remain concealed. He began making fresh guarded inquiries, and learned that the jovial Jacob had taken up a new home with Mrs Polder as soon as Kobus's funeral was over, and from that time she had lived on a more lavish scale. He also learned that prior to his move to The Hague the builder had been free with his money. Ruyter was convinced that van Peit had lived with the widow with an increasingly intimate relationship until he had left Amsterdam. Had he left to escape from her demands? Had Petersen made demands on him? If so, why should he have paid? Ruyter, with the few facts he had, could think of only one explanation. Blackmail. But blackmail about what?

That was where he came back, in his reasoning, to St Peter's and the fatal accident to Kobus Polder. He was also convinced that it was more than coincidence that Petersen should have claimed his back was injured in a similar occupation and at the same place where Mrs Polder's husband had died. There was a natural corollary to his reasoning at this stage.

Had Petersen told him of injuring his back at the church knowing that he would find van Peit and tell him, and so pass on some sort of warning? Certainly van Peit's manner had changed, become a great deal more cautious, when he heard of Petersen's claim.

The inspector next made inquiries among Mrs Polder's neighbours and found he was walking on treacherous ground. He spoke to one woman who did not seem unduly spiteful towards the widow but told him it was common knowledge in the street that she had been over-friendly with Jacob van Peit for a good while before the husband's death.

'Some of us think that's why Mynheer Polder was made a partner,' she said. 'To please the wife.'

Ruyter left the street wondering how much insurance had been taken out to please Mrs Polder in case she was left a widow. It took a little while to find out, but the result was not in the least surprising. Mrs Polder had collected just about enough insurance on her dead husband to pay for a black dress and the funeral expenses.

Ruyter then had inquiries made to check on any other insurance taken out on Kobus Polder's life. This result was much more startling. First, two policies had been taken out by van Peit. One on the life of his partner in Amsterdam for 50,000 guilders, which had been paid under the accidental death clause, and another for 80,000 guilders on the life of his new partner in The Hague. This man's name was Blattner. The second insurance, furthermore, had been taken out in Rotterdam, not The Hague. A possible reason for this was the refusal of the company that had paid out on Polder's death to insure another partner for similar risks.

With this additional knowledge confirming his suspicions about Kobus Polder's death, Ruyter returned for another interview with the widow, who evinced no pleasure at seeing him again. He intended to tell her something in confidence which had just been received by him from the police at The Hague, who had been making inquiries for him.

He penetrated her guard when he said, 'Did you know that Jacob van Peit has taken up with another woman, a night-club singer named Greta Borgmann?'

She jumped up. 'He can't,' she cried. 'He said he'd marry me.'

Ruyter's next question increased her dismay. He asked her if she knew van Peit had taken out life insurance on her husband for the sum of 50,000 guilders.

'No,' she said quickly, 'it was ten thousand.' Then, seeing the look on Ruyter's face, she added, 'He told me after he came here.'

'How much did he give you?' Ruyter wanted to know.

'Not a guilder.' She sounded indignant. Ruyter believed he had broken enough ice. He began to plunge more deeply.

'What can you tell me about van Peit's background. For instance, where did he come from?'

He received another surprise.

'I think he's a German,' she admitted. 'But I can't tell you much about his background and past. He never talked about them. But there is something you can do. Find out what is between him and this Petersen you mentioned last time you were here. I'm sure they have something planned between them.' She paused, frowning. 'At one time Petersen was always calling here for private talks with him. I wasn't allowed in the room, but Petersen left with money in his pocket. Once or twice I saw him folding the notes he'd been given.'

Ruyter asked why Petersen had been paid money, and she said she had no idea, but that she was sure van Peit hated the man. Almost as though he was afraid of him. The inspector could not get her to enlarge on what she had told him, but he extracted a promise from her before he left. If van Peit got in touch with her she would inform the detective.

Ruyter next approached the man being held in custody. He told Petersen that van Peit knew nothing about the other's injured back. The prisoner affected not to believe this piece of news. The detective then told him he was making inquiries about Polder's death.

'That alleged accident was worth fifty thousand guilders to van Peit,' he informed Petersen. 'Now what do you know about it?'

'Nothing.' However, the word came a little too quickly.

Ruyter told the man, who denied knowing anything, that he might be involved in something more serious than burglary, and suggested that Petersen could be helping himself if he remembered what happened the evening of the tragedy.

'Was van Peit at the church at the time?' he asked, point-blank.

Petersen thought over the implications of any answer he made and realized he had to think of himself first.

'He was,' he nodded, and when Ruyter asked how he could be sure said, 'Because I was there with him.'

Ruyter invited the prisoner to relate what had happened that evening. Petersen told him that, after working with Polder, he had climbed down the scaffolding and gone for his cycle. Half-way home, he recalled that he had promised to do a repair job in the house and turned round and rode back to the church where he had left his bag of tools. He had just arrived back in time to hear Polder's hammering stop and the sound of his bucket of stone chippings fall. He was about to grope his way to the foot of the steps when a man detached himself from the shadows and grabbed his throat. The man was van Peit who threatened to kill him if he didn't keep his mouth shut. When the choir came running to see what had happened Petersen was held back in the shadows by the man who had grabbed him. When the hubbub was over and everyone had gone van Peit had taken Petersen back to the builder's office. There van Peit had walked around like a caged lion, grumbling about Polder having been overcome by an attack of dizziness and falling. He had looked at Petersen and seen that his workman did not believe him, though Petersen had said nothing.

Perhaps, Petersen went on with his explanation, that was why van Peit had mentioned some insurance he had on Polder's life. He had professed to be afraid of what the police would think if they knew he was on the scaffold with the dead man. Petersen, according to his account, had told van Peit they should both go to the police and explain precisely what had occurred, but this was instantly vetoed by van Peit, who told his listener that he would 'fix' him if he opened his mouth and told what he knew.

When Petersen asked what he meant van Peit had said threateningly, 'I'll tell the police you hated Polder and had quarrelled with him and sworn to get him, and I came to the church in time to see you strike him so that he fell from the top of the scaffold.'

What he had just been told could be the truth. Ruyter had to be sure.

'How much did he pay you as the price of your silence?' he asked.

'He offered to keep me in funds for a year.'

Ruyter switched back to Polder on the scaffold. What light did the stonemason have as it grew dark? A naked electric bulb on a long flex, Petersen told him. The light was burning when he left on his bike, but not when he returned, which is why he hadn't seen van Peit in the shadows. He also said van Peit had dropped something in the canal as they went to the office. It was an object which fell in the water with a heavy plopping sound.

'Could you show me where?' the detective inquired.

'Yes.'

In this, at least, Petersen had told the truth. Ruyter had the canal dredged at that spot and a stonemason's hammer was recovered from the canal's bottom.

Ruyter, now sure of murder, made inquiries in the vicinity of St Peter's and found a family named Jurgens who occupied a flat overlooking the churchyard. After the police and firemen had left the husband saw two figures hurrying away. Although Mynheer Jurgens didn't think he would be able to recognize either of those figures in daylight, his story lent support to Petersen's latest account of what happened.

Ruyter next approached the German police. He had secretly obtained van Peit's fingerprints and a copy was sent with his request for information. It took some time but at length word came back – from Hamburg, where a man named Weiner had been jailed for fraud in 1935. This meant that the angry widow had been right. Van Peit was Weiner, a German.

The man Ruyter believed to be the murderer of Polder was brought back to Amsterdam and told that his Dutch citizen's papers were a forgery. Van Peit flew into a temper, but his rage evaporated when Ruyter shared the knowledge he had obtained from Germany.

'What are you going to do?' van Peit asked. He looked as though his jovial bulk had in some way crumpled inside.

'I'm arresting you for murder.'

'You're trying to scare me,' the arrested man said in his perfect Dutch.

'I think I shall succeed,' Ruyter said quietly.

Jacob van Peit did not return to The Hague or to his new partner, Hermann Blattner, a refugee from Nazi Germany who had no knowledge that he had been insured for 80,000 guilders with a company in Rotterdam. He was kept in Amsterdam and charged in his lawful name of Gottfried Weiner, while Inspector Ruyter, a detective who had been working overtime on this case, went to make arrangements for the final phase – the re-enactment of the crime at St Peter's. This was done without informing the newspapers, for Ruyter did not require an audience willing to be entertained by a thoroughly macabre situation.

Reconstruction of a murder scene is commonplace on the Continent, particularly in France, where it is normal procedure for a Sûreté detective. It is much less common in England, although occasionally it is considered valuable in an investigation. For instance, it had happened during Superintendent Francis Carlin's inquiry into the murder of Mrs Buxton, the licensee of the Cross Keys public house in Chelsea in 1920, nearly a score of years before Inspector Ruyter held his reconstruction of a crime at Bylderdyk.

But whereas Carlin, who was another of Scotland Yard's original 'Big Four', like Arthur Neil, failed in Chelsea, the painstaking Dutchman had better fortune with his grim little drama at St Peter's of a crime committed more than a year before.

At the start of the reconstruction the prisoner was brazen and contemptuous, but his attitude changed drastically when Wilhelm Petersen was produced by a couple of plain-clothes Criminal Police. Weiner knew then that his accomplice, bought with threats and cash, had turned on him. Against such a witness he had no hope of glibly talking his way out of trouble.

When the reconstruction was over Ruyter had his case sewn up. The man he had charged with murder of Kobus Polder had no answer that could free him. He went to jail and in due course appeared before the Dutch court and heard the evidence against him delivered in a terrible tone of conviction.

Gottfried Weiner went back to prison from the court after a final glimpse of a face that looked like a stranger's. It belonged to Kobus Polder's widow. The only moment she had seemed pleased was when she heard the verdict of 'Guilty' delivered.

8 WHAT THE
LITTLE DOG FOUND

At three o'clock on a misty November day in 1943 a car left Scotland Yard for St Pancras station, about three miles away. It was conveying two members of the Murder Squad with their 'murder bag' on the first stage of a journey to Luton, thirty miles to the north of London. The train they caught at St Pancras drew into the station at Midland Road, Luton, a few minutes after four o'clock. Another car was waiting to take them to an interview with the Chief Constable of Bedfordshire.

The Chief Constable had a sheaf of reports to hand over to Bill Chapman and he told him, ' I've had an office put at your disposal, chief inspector.'

Chief Inspector William Chapman and his assistant, Sergeant W. Judge, moved in and from that moment Scotland Yard was responsible for finding the person who had thrown the body of an unknown woman into the River Lea. The few first-hand reports so far obtained did not amount to much. Earlier two men on their way to work had noticed something floating near the river's bank and because it was apparently tied up in sacking they dragged the bundle ashore, tore it open, and received a shock.

The bundle had contained the body of a woman whose face was badly battered, as though someone had deliberately tried to make it unrecognizable. Moreover, there were no clothes on the corpse. The body was naked.

The police had been informed. A surgeon had made a post-mortem examination and local detectives had examined clothes that had been found stuffed into a separate small sack. False teeth had been removed from the woman's mouth, presumably before her face had been so brutally disfigured. The body had been found with the ankles tied and the knees caught up to the stomach by a cord that went round the victim's waist.

Dr Keith Simpson was asked to examine the body. He said afterwards she was a woman about thirty-five. She had borne children and at the time she was found was some six months' pregnant.

But who was she? That was a question to which no answer would be found until some months had passed. Bill Chapman started examining the bank of the river from which the body had been taken. The search continued for two miles in the hope of finding a clue that would point to where the body was dumped. The search drew a blank.

He decided that the case warranted a house-to-house inquiry in the town. The condition of the dead woman's hands suggested that she came from a working-class background. He had a team of police call at houses in the back streets. While they were obtaining answers to their questionnaire, Chapman and Judge went through files of women reported missing in South Bedfordshire. Later this part of the investigation extended into North Hertfordshire. In this way four hundred and four women were traced.

Medical evidence had established that the woman had died about twenty-four hours before she was found in the sacking. The badly disfigured face was treated and built up so that a reasonable photograph could be taken. Copies were distributed to the press. Lantern slides were made and distributed to the cinematograph trade. The face that had appeared in newspapers reappeared on the screen of cinemas in the South of England with the following announcement:

MURDER
Police are still anxious
to establish the identity of
this unfortunate woman.
Here is her picture.
If any person can help please
communicate with the police immediately.

This publicity did not result in the police learning the identity of the murdered woman, but it did help in finding missing women whose absence had been worrying their families. Forty persons wanted to be sure the dead woman was not someone missing from their family circle.

The police inquiry was directed to the factories in the Luton and Dunstable region. Two hundred and fifty lorry drivers who called at the Vauxhall factory site, which is not far from where the body in the sack was recovered from the River Lea, were questioned. As it was wartime basic foodstuffs were rationed, and shops were visited in the hope that someone had withdrawn a woman's ration card which might provide a clue.

Then the letters began arriving from overseas. Hundreds of them, all sent by Servicemen who had seen the newspaper reports and were anxious to know if the dead woman could be a wife or fiancée.

All such letters had to be dealt with, the Servicemen's womenfolk contacted, and replies sent to the anxious men overseas. The letter inquiries produced nothing helpful.

Nor did the police inquiry that was spreading, with the passing weeks, to other towns, including St Albans, Welwyn, and Letchworth. The number of lorry drivers interviewed grew to a thousand, and all the reports flowing in were sent to Chapman. One of the few statistics lacking in the case is the number of fresh ounces of tobacco the Yard chief inspector smoked during those dark winter days! The house-to-house inquiry fizzled out after providing mounds of paperwork. Yet all the time the area of inquiry grew until it had spread hundreds of miles from Bedfordshire to cover all of Britain and even the Irish Republic.

From distant parts came six letters informing Chapman that the writer had reason to believe the dead woman was a relative who had been missing from home for a long time. It took up much time dealing with these suggestions. When they had been dealt with Chapman still did not know the woman's identity.

He and Judge were working most hours of day and night, and when he was recalled to Scotland Yard for consultation with his superiors he was a disappointed man. But not a disheartened one. He told the men who listened to his report, 'This is a case that will break suddenly.'

'How can you be sure?' he was asked.

'I have that feeling.'

He returned to Luton still with that feeling – and a new idea. If the woman's clothes that had been left at home had been sold a second-hand clothes shop might hold a clue. Or if they had been burned and discarded, some rubbish dump might hold a clue. These were two chances he could not afford to ignore.

The men working under his direction began roaming around the waste spaces in and around Luton. Others called on second-hand clothes dealers. The dead woman's clothes that had been rammed into a sack with the body had been freshly cleaned after careful forensic examination. They were used to suggest to dealers the kind of clothes that might have been in her wardrobe. But the new lines of investigation brought no positive result.

Christmas came and January passed with Chapman and Judge still finding fresh sources of inquiry, new faces to interview, additional mounds of reports to go through. Locally and back in Scotland Yard there were changing opinions.

'This will be another of those unsolved crimes the newspaper reporters like to write about,' said one official, but not in Chapman's hearing, though he heard of it later.

If the Murder Squad detective realized that some of his colleagues were losing faith in his eventually solving the case he gave no sign. He might have expressed some bitterness to Judge, but if he did the detective sergeant was a man who knew how to keep his tongue silent. Moreover, he was very loyal to his immediate chief, whom he understood as well as anyone who ever worked with Bill Chapman.

So the investigation continued, patiently, doggedly, in the face of complete absence of clue or encouragement. Then it was that Chapman's feeling of two months before came to be justified and was proved to be an inspired insight rather than mere wishful thinking, as so many had come to believe. It was in February that the break Chapman had been waiting for came to change the tempo of the inquiry and allow him to close a solved murder case.

Years later my old friend Chief Superintendent Fred Cherrill, who was chief of Scotland Yard's Fingerprint Bureau before his retirement, wrote of the Luton body in a sack :

The case was as near the perfect murder as can be imagined. The slayer took infinite pains to cover up his tracks in order to elude justice. He did not succeed, however. What led to his undoing was a very prosaic object – a pickle bottle. On it was a thumbprint of the victim, and it was this mark that finally established the identity of the murdered woman and led to the solution of one of the most intriguing mysteries I have ever been engaged on.

However, before that pickle bottle was found for Fred Cherrill to test for fingerprints, Chapman had a curious and almost fiction-like encounter with a dog. It happened at a time when even the persevering chief inspector was gloomily envisaging the possibility of having to retire with the case not officially closed, which would be a personal defeat for him.

He voiced his doubts as he walked with Sergeant Judge through some of the back streets he had come to know fairly well. They turned a corner and walked along a street of red-brick terrace houses with slate roofs and no front gardens, for the houses emptied on to the front pavement. Some way down the street was a piece of waste ground that was littered with sundry kinds of refuse that looked dismal after being soaked with winter rain and sleet. As they drew level with the waste ground Chapman surprised his companion by stopping short.

Judge saw that his chief was watching a small dog that was jumping about on the waste ground. He had a piece of soiled rag in his mouth and was trying to jump at it.

When Chapman, followed by Judge, walked towards him the dog stopped jumping up and down and ran around in circles, barking and pawing at the piece of rag still gripped in its teeth. Every now and then the dog paused to look at them and bark.

'He's laughing at us,' Chapman said, grinning.

They stood watching the capering dog until Chapman said abruptly, 'I want that piece of cloth.'

The two Yard men moved together. They caught the dog and removed the cloth from its jaws. It was filthy and discoloured, but it had obviously been part of a female garment, probably an overcoat. Chapman returned to the police station that had been turned into his local headquarters and smoothed out the rag on his desk. The dog's teeth marks were plain. But the little dog had not made the ragged edges with stretched and twisted threads of cloth. The piece of cloth had obviously been torn from a larger piece. In fact, the more Chapman examined his not very savoury find the more he was certain that the cloth was part of a sleeve that had been ripped from a shoulder joint. There was a piece of filthy lining screwed up at one end. He straightened this out and found a shoulder pad. This in turn had a number on it.

When he had washed and rinsed the piece of cloth he found he could read the number. It was V.I.2247.

'This is part of a sleeve from a coat that was dyed,' he informed his sergeant and pointed to the number. 'This is a dyer's number.'

The next day a fresh inquiry began, this time at the shops of cleaners and dyers. Sure enough the number Chapman had found inside the little dog's rag was also shown to be entered in the books of a local firm. A coat had been left to be dyed black. The person who had brought the coat to the firm was a Mrs Manton of Regent Street, Luton. Regent Street was the street with the piece of waste ground on which the little dog had been playing. Chapman went to the house and met her husband and a little girl who bore a strong resemblance to the woman he had been trying to identify for three months.

'I'm Bertie Manton,' said the man. 'What do you want?'

'I'd like a word with your wife, Mr Manton,' Chapman said quietly.

'Well, she's not home. Matter of fact, Caroline's away with friends in London.'

With Chapman and Judge watching him, the man produced some letters which he claimed he had received from her. Chapman held out his hand and reluctantly, it seemed, they were given to him. Chapman looked at the writing on the sheets of paper and saw that they contained little of interest or news, except for a misspelling. The address at the head of the letter was in Hampstead. But the place-name on the sheet of paper Chapman was looking at was written 'Hamstead'. He looked at the dates on the letters and found they ranged in time from December, before Christmas, until just a few days before in February.

'She's staying away a long time,' he said.

Bertie Manton fidgeted. 'Well, to tell the truth, she's left me and she's got a job in London somewhere. But she still writes.'

A very convenient habit, Chapman considered, for obviously a woman who had been dead couldn't still be writing. Chapman was about to take his leave when there was a bark outside the door and the sound of a dog tapping at the woodwork with a paw. Manton opened the door. The little black and white mongrel that had been playing with the rag on the waste ground bounded into the room. It ran to Chapman and licked his hand as it stood wagging its tail.

'Yours?' he asked Manton.

The man nodded.

Chapman left. Back in the police station he rang the Yard and spoke to Fred Cherrill.

'You'd better come down here, Fred,' he said, 'and give the place a going over.'

So the chief of the Fingerprint Bureau arrived in Luton some hours later with his portable equipment. He was taken to the Manton home in Regent Street and started work in the kitchen. Pots and pans, glasses and cups, cutlery, ornaments, and wall pictures were tested. There wasn't a fingerprint on anything. It was as though they had all been carefully wiped clean very recently. Cherrill invaded other rooms and cupboards, made his way over shelves and in corners, still without finding a fingerprint. The lack of a fingerprint was not only unusual. It was fantastic. But he kept at the work hopefully. He found a small cellar-like place under the stairs and rigged up a torch to provide light. The place was filmed with unbroken layers of dust. At the back was a shelf covered with many kinds of bottles, ranging from jam jars to beer bottles and medicine bottles. What intrigued Cherrill was that none of the bottles on the dusty shelf was dusty. He worked his way along that shelf of bottles. All were free of fingerprints. He was about to withdraw when a movement of his head allowed a chink of light to reach to a far corner of the shelf that he couldn't see from his former position. In that overlooked corner he found another bottle, the last on the shelf. It was filmed with dust, so he knew someone else had overlooked it besides himself. He said later:

It was a pickle bottle. I handled it carefully, almost lovingly, for this was my last hope. It was the one remaining article in the whole of that house which had not been tested, and it was the one remaining article which the murderer somehow overlooked when, in his anxiety to remove all traces of his crime, he had carefully performed his cleaning operations.

This bottle had not been cleaned like the others. On its sloping shoulders was a film of dust. I tested it and knew at once that this prosaic article held the secret which had eluded the police for three months, the secret which they were so anxious to discover – the identity of the body in the sack.

A single thumbprint on that pickle bottle corresponded to a print of the dead woman's in the set that had been sent to Cherrill months earlier.

Meantime a check in North London proved that Caroline Manton was not known there. Sure that the dead woman was Bertie Manton's wife, Chapman joined the husband in a room of the house in Regent Street and asked him to write a short message. Looking a little surprised by such a request, the man nodded and wrote at Chapman's dictation. One of the words in the message was the place name Hampstead.

When Chapman read what Manton had written he found the place name written as 'Hamstead'.

Chapman told him that he believed the woman in the sack was his wife and asked him to make a statement. There was no way out for a man who had been trapped by his own actions and who didn't know that the trap had been sprung by his own dog.

He started his statement by telling Chapman he had done what he had for the sake of his children because all his wife had wanted was a good time. She had neglected the home and the children. 'Will you please do the best you can for them?' he asked plaintively.

The actual confession to the crime began when he said, 'I killed her, but it was only because I lost my temper. I didn't intend to.' He went on to explain how he had four days' leave from his job of driving a lorry for the National Fire Service in November. He had induced his wife to return for the sake of the children, and it was 18 November, when they were finishing their tea, that he said he would be going to a public house where he was known to give them a hand, as he put it. His wife had found an excuse in this to lose her temper. She threw at him a cup of tea she had just poured out. That was when his temper followed hers, only more violently. He picked up a heavy stool and hit her over the head several times. In the statement he related:

'When I came to and got my senses again I saw what I'd done. I saw she was dead, and decided I had to do something to keep her away from the children. I undressed her and got four sacks from the cellar, cut them open, and tied her up in them. I carried her down the cellar and left her there.'

He explained how he disposed of the body.

'I had washed up the blood before the children came home to tea. I hid the bloodstained clothing in a corner near the copper. After tea Ivy went out with a friend, and the two boys and Sheila went to the pictures. After it was dark I brought the wife up from the cellar, got my bike out, laid her across the handlebars, and wheeled her down to the river. I laid her on the edge of the bank, and she rolled into the river.'

Bertie Manton certainly didn't look to be a man of the stuff one imagines murderers are made of. But then there is no such being as a ready-made murderer unless that description is applied to everyone. He was not a big-framed man. Indeed, he was rather sparely built, and in earlier years had been a light-weight boxer without gaining any distinction in the ring. In manner and appearance he seemed a mild man, slightly apologetic. He was a good father to his children according to his lights. He had received little more than a rudimentary education and in the labour market of his day could earn barely enough to keep and support his growing family. Money had been a constant worry and the lack of it a reproach he had seldom been able to avoid.

His greatest misfortune was that he had married a woman who had not been satisfied with trying to make the most of her marriage. She saw her children as an incubus, keeping her in the house when she much preferred to be in a public house or a dance-hall, enjoying the company of attentive males. Not surprisingly such a woman in time came to resent her husband for his social inadequacies. She went out to work and finally saw the chance to break away from a life that held no remaining attraction for her. Manton had been able to get her to return to the little dingy house in Regent Street from time to time. But after a few days she would not consider remaining any longer. Her husband kept hoping for a change. The change did not come, except for the worse.

All this was made manifest when later that year Manton stood trial at Bedford Assizes for the murder of his wife. By that time Bill Chapman had been able to produce additional pieces of evidence to support his own case and the prisoner's confession.

He had checked Manton's leave dates with a record of rotas at the local National Fire Service headquarters and found that these in each case coincided with the dates on the letters allegedly written by his wife and with the postmarks on the envelopes. In short, Manton had on each occasion gone to North London to post the letter written to himself.

Unfortunately for him he was a poor speller.

Chapman, during a closer examination of the house in Regent Street after Manton's arrest, had found a single speck of dried blood concealed in the door jamb of the room where husband and wife spent their last tea-time together. That speck was flaked off with a knife and sent to be tested. It proved to be of blood group O, the same group as Caroline Manton's.

Arthur Ward, KC, did his spirited best for Manton during the trial in Bedford, trying to argue that the crime was not truly one of murder but rather of manslaughter, and had resulted from sharp provocation, with no hint of premeditation. The whole tragic business had been a spur-of-the-moment affair.

To an extent the answers of Chapman when he appeared in the witness box for the Crown supported the defence's picture of Manton's unfortunate background and unhappy marriage, and the detective who later became the head of the Murder Squad as Superintendent Chapman agreed that Bertie Manton had been a man of good character who was devoted to his children.

But his story of the subterfuges employed by Manton, added to the testimony of Dr Keith Simpson, the Home Office pathologist who had journeyed from London to examine the body taken from the soggy bundle of sacking, left the jury visibly impressed.

When Richard O'Sullivan, KC, cross-examined Manton for the prosecution he forced the prisoner to make an admission which impressed the jury even further.

Speaking of Caroline Manton, the Crown counsel asked the prisoner, 'She was quite a small woman?'

'About my size, sir. A little shade bigger,' Manton replied.

'No match for you in strength?'

'No, sir.'

'Did you hear Dr Keith Simpson tell the jury that there were marks upon the neck of application of a hand and re-application of a hand?'

'Yes, sir. I remember holding her throat and pushing her against the wall.'

'And that the marks showed that the hand had been applied with considerable force?'

Manton hesitated, considering his reply, perhaps aware of where it would lead him.

He did not answer directly, but said, 'I may have grabbed her twice, but that was in my temper.'

Then came the really destructive question.

'You said nothing about that in your statement to the police?'

Another moment of hesitation and then the damaging admission, 'No, sir.'

The jury, after receiving legal instruction from Mr Justice Singleton on the difference between manslaughter and murder, retired and eventually returned with a verdict of 'Guilty'.

Not long afterwards the death sentence was commuted to one of penal servitude, and Bertie Manton was sent to Parkhurst, in the Isle of Wight, to serve his sentence. But he did not live long after the tragedy that had wrecked a number of lives. He was taken ill suddenly in November 1947 and died within a few days.

There was tragedy, too, in Chapman's own family. After his

death, which followed Manton's in less than eight years, his son, Frederick James Chapman, a married schoolmaster living in Kent, was in August 1955 arrested for murdering his wife and daughter with a hammer. At Maidstone Assizes in the following November he was found guilty but insane and was sentenced to be detained during Her Majesty's pleasure. Dr John Matheson, the medical officer of Brixton Prison, told the Kent jury that William Chapman, the father, had 'set a very high standard for his son, and I think the son thought he was failing his father.' Dr Matheson thought the prisoner was suffering from acute melancholia at the time of the crime and did not know he was doing wrong.

It was a grim final curtain of a kind few authors would dare to ring down on a play or a novel.

9 BORROWED FROM FICTION

However, if the tragedy that occurred in Bill Chapman's family is not likely to be a theme borrowed by a writer of fiction, there is on record an example of a murderer in real life deliberately following a crime worked out in a novel. As such it is a rare case and worthy of inclusion with other cases that occurred in the present century, for it offered the police of the time a baffling mystery. This remarkable murder case occurred in Germany a little short of twenty years before the nineteenth century closed.

The setting is Berlin. It opened on a day in 1881 when a patrolling policeman in a Berlin working-class suburb heard someone calling to him. He turned and saw a man waving an arm to attract his attention. As the policeman turned about and retraced his steps in the direction of the obviously agitated man he took stock of the other.

He saw a thickset working man in stained everyday clothes, with run-over boots that had little shine. The man had a square face that could have been more closely shaved, and his cap with a cracked peak was drawn well down over small beady eyes that seemed about to burst from his face with suppressed excitement.

'What's the matter?' asked the policeman as he drew within normal speaking distance of the excited workman.

The man was still waving an arm.

'Something's wrong,' he said. 'I can't get into my apartment.'

The policeman surveyed the other with cold eyes, as though he suspected him of perpetrating a very poor joke. He frowned to register his disapproval.

'What's that supposed to mean?' he asked. 'You've come out without your key or you've lost it?'

The workman thrust a grubby hand into a pocket and produced a small latch-key. He waved it to and fro before the policeman's face.

'This is my key. I've been home and tried to get in with it, but I can't. The door is bolted on the inside. I tell you something's wrong,' he repeated. 'I want some help to get indoors.'

The policeman's manner changed. After all, this could be a joke, but against the odd character with the cloth cap and choked-up voice.

'You should knock louder on the door,' he advised, beginning to look amused for the first time at the man's plight. 'Ten to one your wife's asleep and doesn't intend to be disturbed. You'll have to change her ideas, won't you?'

The kerbside badinage was of a kind the policeman enjoyed. It made up for the hours of pounding pavements and wearing out shoe leather. Such a verbal exchange broke the monotony of the average spell of duty and gave him something to talk about later and win a few laughs of appreciation. But the cloth-capped workman didn't look as though he could share the policeman's amusement.

'Look,' he said, 'I've hammered on the door and I've called to her. It makes no difference. She doesn't answer. There's not a sound from inside, but if the door's bolted she must be home. So something's happened to her.'

The policeman saw that his few moments of fun at the workman's expense were over. The man expected him to do something.

'What makes you so sure?' he asked.

'I said there wasn't a sound after my banging and shouting. Well there should have been. I've got five kids. They should have been yelling.'

The policeman took out his notebook and became excessively official. He didn't like this talk of five silent children.

'First, let's have your name.'

'Conrad. Look, officer, I only live round the corner.'

'Address?'

When told the policeman wrote it down, also the time, and

some few lines to remind himself that the man had shown him a key. Then he put his notebook away and became brisk in manner.

'Very well, Herr Conrad, let's go and see why you can't get into your home.'

But when he arrived at the apartment in a working-class block of tenements he had no more success than Conrad. He shouted to Frau Conrad that it was the police at the door and asked her to open it. There was no reply and no movement that he could hear from the landing where neighbours appeared, brought to their doors by the noise. When he banged on the door the silence on the far side remained unbroken.

'Wait here,' he told Conrad. 'I've got to report this. If it means breaking the door down we'll have to get permission from the landlord. You understand?'

'Can you hurry?' Conrad urged.

'I'll do my best. Now don't go away.'

As soon as the policeman had gone gossiping housewives besieged the man who couldn't get into his home. He listened to their chatter, nodding occasionally, but he volunteered nothing that could be described as information. All he would say was he couldn't get into his apartment because the door was bolted.

Eventually the landlord was found and his permission to force the door open received. More policemen arrived, followed by men from a building firm, who, under direction from the superior of the officer who had reported the bolted door, proceeded to lever the door from its jamb, so that the hinges could be removed. The removal of the hinges still left the door something of a barrier to be forced and the reason was found when workmen and police squeezed their way past the tilted door, kept in that position by the bolt. The bolt had been kept well oiled so that it moved easily, and it had been pushed all the way in its metal groove.

A terrible sight met the horrified gazes of the intruders into her home. Hanging by a short length of rope from a hook fixed in one corner of the living-room was a middle-aged woman with seamed face, the lower part of which was sagging unpleasantly. There were streaks of grey in her hair. The clothes draped on her body were of poor quality and some of them threadbare.

Her shoes were run down and one was broken. The nails on the fingers protruding from her sleeves were worn down from continuous work. She had a peasant's face that was now a faint shade of blue.

The police officer in charge of the invasion turned to Conrad, who was staring at the woman's hanging corpse as though fascinated by it.

'This is your wife?'

Conrad appeared to rouse himself. 'Yes,' he nodded, and walked a few steps to a chair. He sat down, still staring at the woman on the end of the short rope. He might have been seeing her for the first time.

'Where are the children?'

Conrad shook his head dazedly. 'They must be here. She wouldn't have sent them out.'

But there were no children in the small apartment – until one of the policemen opened the door of a large cupboard built against a wall of the room where the family had slept. The door was closed with a simple drop-latch. When it was opened the policeman exclaimed aloud with horror. His companions came to stare at what he had discovered. It was an even more terrible sight than had confronted them in the living-room.

Hanging from ordinary cupboard hooks, as though they were garments, were five small bodies. The face of each dead child was pinched and tinged with an even deeper shade of blue than the mother's. They were removed and it was found that the rope around the necks of two had almost disappeared into the flesh. Placed on the floor, the sight was truly pathetic, for the children did not look robust. They were thin and dressed in clothes that were almost rags. They presented a shocking picture of abject poverty.

A police doctor was summoned. When he arrived he examined the pathetic row of small bodies and then went to the room where the mother's body had been kept apart. While the doctor made his examination Conrad remained seated in the chair near his wife's body. He said nothing and sat staring like a man in shock, as he well might be.

He made no move until he heard the police officer in charge addressing the medical man.

' Would you say there is any doubt, Herr Doktor?'

Conrad watched the frowning doctor shake his head.

' I should say there is no room for any doubt whatever,' the doctor replied. ' The poor woman strangled her children and then did away with herself. She must have been emotionally overwrought and despondent. You can see the kind of struggle she had. Five mouths to feed and I'd say they didn't get enough to eat, though the husband doesn't look starved.'

Suddenly Conrad was conscious of many eyes observing him, and the gaze of all was critical. A couple of the police came over to him and began asking questions. Had he quarrelled with his wife? He shook his head and muttered that life hadn't been easy with so many mouths to feed and wages low. Was his wife more upset than usual? Again he gave a head shake and said not more than was normal. She was a woman who let things get on top of her too easily.

At that comment the mouths of his questioners tightened.

' Do you owe money?' he was asked.

He appeared to think of what the question might imply, and finally said, ' To some shopkeepers. We've always owed some of them something, ever since the first kid came.'

It was tragic and it was extremely pitiful, but in 1881 it was not a unique story for a policeman to hear. In different tongues it was being told in most big cities of Europe and even in some in the United States. But there was a twist to the present story of six deaths that at the time was not suspected.

The police had the bodies removed to the local mortuary and the landlord sent his own workmen to repair the forced door. Before the police left the tenements Conrad was asked to call in at the police station and make a formal statement for the records.

The man whose life had presumably been stripped bare by the swift removal of his wife and five children showed a readiness to go with the police and lose no time. The door was still being fixed when he left with them. At the police station he was kept waiting for some time, then he was shown into the office of the local commissioner, Herr Hollmann, who was a keen student of his fellow-men and their behaviour – in particular of their mis-behaviour.

He had run through the doctor's first report and the early report made out by the policeman who had been summoned by Conrad. He asked Conrad some additional questions and these fresh answers were added to another form. Once the commissioner was ready to receive him Conrad's visit did not take very long. When he dismissed the man Herr Hollmann said, 'They'll tell you outside where you can get assistance with the funeral expenses.'

The bereaved man, who had told the commissioner that he drove a cart for a living, gave a bobbing little bow and shuffled out of the tidy office his presence had seemed to soil. He left behind him when the door closed a puzzled police official who was struggling to understand his own antipathy to the grubby man he had just questioned. Herr Hollmann had been deeply disturbed by the terrible tragedy. He could understand the dead woman's despair at the continued bleak outlook for her family, but not the overthrow of all maternal instinct that resulted in an act of savage brutality to the children she had borne. To Herr Hollmann this seemed inexplicable, and yet it had happened. His tidy and logical Teutonic mind accepted that something had happened which had made life desperately unbearable, and presumably it had happened while the husband was away from his family.

He sent for the first policeman to speak to the carter.

'I want you to make discreet inquiries around that block of tenements,' he told the man. 'Find out all you can about this Conrad family. I want neighbours' opinions, even possible scandal. But don't let anyone suspect you're acting officially.'

Two days later the man reported. What he told Herr Hollmann caused the police chief to scowl. He didn't like the piece about the neighbours believing Conrad had purposely kept his wife short of money. Conrad was known to be a lazy man and no one had much of an opinion of him. He was shiftless and frequently out of work. Yet he had a very good opinion of himself.

The mother had done her best in an impossible situation that never improved, and there had been times when she had to listen to her children crying with hunger, especially when Conrad had been away from home. No one on these occasions knew where he had gone. It was generally supposed he had got work with a haulage contractor outside the German capital. But the job had never lasted long. One detail the policeman had brought was of particular interest to the police chief.

'He's always reading,' one of the neighbours had said. 'Whenever he's been home it wasn't to help his wife. It was to settle down with his nose in a book.'

Herr Hollman consulted the doctor and afterwards went through the reports to discover anything he could find that might point to the dead woman's state of mind. There was no suggestion from any quarter that Frau Conrad's mind could possibly have been deranged. She had not made friends. In fact, she had not mixed very much with her neighbours. But that was understandable if she had felt keenly ashamed of the family's poverty.

But Herr Hollmann had found his first inconsistency and it plagued him. Conrad was a reader. He enjoyed books. Then why had the man presented himself as a veritable clod. Hollmann required the answer to two urgent questions. Was Conrad a deep man with a shrewdness he concealed effectively? And what kind of books did he read?

The police chief decided he had best secure the answers for himself or he might start too many tongues wagging among his own men. He called at the Conrad flat in the middle of the day and stood for a time inspecting the repaired door. Inside he gave his close attention to the few sticks of rickety furniture that had been the family's total of possessions. On a shelf he found a few tattered books. He was not impressed by them. They were sensational novels. Conrad had probably read them as a means of escaping the boredom of his restricted and shabby life.

He went back to the door, for that was where his real interest focused. He closed it and shot the bolt, and satisfied himself there was no means of entry with the door bolted on the inside. The windows were set well above street level and almost flush with the outside of the wall. He paced the few rooms of the apartment. It seemed impossible that there could be a solution other than the obvious – Frau Conrad had killed her children and then herself. He went back to the landing door and worked the well-oiled lock as though handling the bolt with his fingers would start some fresh idea taking shape in his mind. His mind remained an annoying blank.

The next day Conrad had to appear at the police station to fill in some forms that were purely a technical municipal procedure. Herr Hollman observed the carter without the man being aware of the interest he had aroused in the police chief. He thought he had found a new smugness in the bereaved man who should not have recovered fully from shock. The police chief came to the conclusion that the man seemed different because now he was no longer wearing a mask over his emotions. He thoroughly distrusted the smug man who had lost his family in frightful circumstances, and took a fast decision as Conrad was on the point of leaving.

'I want you to follow that man,' he told a detective. 'Report to me how he spends his time and where.'

When the man made his report Herr Hollmann learned that Conrad was interested in a servant girl who lived in another part of Berlin. She was younger than Conrad, had a bold manner and a local reputation for being no better than she should be.

'From what I've been told,' the detective informed his chief, 'Conrad has been spending money on her for some while.'

The police chief looked angry. It was a sordid story. A man starving his family so that he could win the favour of a younger woman than his wife.

'Have you found out what he got for his money?'

'Letters. That's about all, sir.'

'What do you mean letters?'

'This girl writes to him regularly. Love letters, I expect.'

The next day, while Conrad was at work, Herr Hollmann and this detective visited the Conrad tenement, and to a puzzled companion the police chief said, 'We're looking for those love letters you mentioned, so don't let's waste time.'

They found none. Whatever letters Conrad had received from the young woman were not in the apartment. If he had not burned them they were hidden elsewhere. As a last resource the police chief ran through the pages of the shelf of novels. He found no letters, but he did notice that one book opened naturally at a certain page, as though it had been pressed open at that place because someone had wanted to read it several times.

The book was a novel by an English writer whose name on the title-page was John Radcliffe. The title of the book conveyed little to a German. It was *Nena Sahib*. Intrigued, the police chief began to read the passage where the book fell open naturally. To his amazement, he was reading about a suicide in a locked room. He turned to the opening of the story and began to skip through the novel. Apparently the man believed to have committed suicide was a rich Indian living in London. He was found by his servants dead in a locked room. The room had been locked by sliding a bolt on the inside.

When the dead man was discovered his death was accepted as suicide until an English private detective solved an incredible mystery by discovering a tiny hole that had been pierced in the woodwork of the door near the bolt. Through this hole a strand of wire could be passed. With one end twisted into a loop and hooked over the handle of the bolt, it was possible to bolt or unbolt the door on the inside by using the wire on the outside. The English detective had found the small hole for the wire filled in with putty.

Herr Hollmann didn't need to finish the novel. He turned to the impatient detective and told him, 'I want this door removed and brought to my office. Get some workmen. If the landlord objects bring him to my office with his door.'

A couple of hours later Herr Hollmann was bending over the door, which was lying across his desk. He found a small nodule near the door's edge a few inches from the bolt on the other side. He pared away this nodule with a sharp-bladed knife, and the pieces were examined and found to be tinted sealing wax. A packing needle was pushed through the exposed hole and the wax filling removed. Adhering to some of the wax particles were strands of horsehair.

A man who drove a horse and cart and was around stables for a part of each day would naturally have horsehair on his clothes. It would be just as natural for him to remove a few such strands and use them to penetrate a tiny hole he had made in a door. They would be silent and he could leave them embedded in the wax.

In its way the horsehair was an improvement on fiction. For had Conrad used a piece of wire and it had slipped from his grasp at the last moment it would have fallen on the inside of the door and provided a piece of evidence that would convict him. The horsehair was much safer, being almost invisible at first glance. In any case, all Conrad had to do after using a loop made of horsehair strands was to wait until the police had gone, fill the tiny hole with sealing wax and rub it down, then tint the wax on each side of the hole to match the door.

Certain that he had solved a rare kind of murder mystery, Herr Hollmann wanted to be sure he could prove his theory. He sent a policeman to procure some horsehair, which he twisted into a single thin-stranded rope with a loop at one end. He had to experiment several times before the horsehair had the right amount of rigidity to enable him to move the bolt caught in the loop he had made. He knew then why it had been necessary to oil the bolt.

He knew something else. The action of drawing the horsehair through the small hole that was not smooth inside had severed a few of the strands. That was how he had come to find the strands adhering to the wax scraps he had removed from the hole.

He was just about finished when he had a very annoyed visitor. It was Conrad, who had been told where his door had gone by neighbours in the tenement building.

' I want my door,' he shouted.

However, when he saw the door on the police chief's desk he became strangely silent, a man with no words he could trust himself to speak.

' You can have your door, Herr Conrad,' the police chief told him, ' after your trial and if you are acquitted.'

Conrad had suddenly lost his smugness as well as his indignation. He stood in the police chief's office trembling.

' What's this about a trial?' he forced himself to say. ' I don't understand.'

' I think you do,' said Herr Hollmann. ' The bolted door was a clever way of providing yourself with an alibi. You murdered your wife and children.' The police chief paused, frowning at the man he had defeated. ' Why did you have to get rid of all of them?'

Conrad stumbled to a chair and sat down.

'She insisted on marriage,' he said, like a man talking to himself. He did not say of whom he was talking, but Herr Hollmann did not need to inquire. 'It was marriage or she wouldn't see me again,' he added miserably. 'I couldn't bear the thought of that. I was in love with her.'

'For that one young woman you murdered six, your wife and your own children, and you did it brutally.'

Conrad looked at the speaker as though he had not heard the last words.

'There was no other way,' he insisted. 'She told me it must be marriage or we wouldn't see each other again.'

'When did she tell you?'

'She put it in the letters she wrote.'

Herr Hollmann stared at the wretched carter. So the letters had not been love letters, as his detective had supposed. Or at least not the kind of love letters the average young woman sends to a man who has told her he loves her.

'And you destroyed these letters?'

Conrad's head jerked upright on his shoulders. 'Of course,' he exclaimed as though surprised by the question. 'I couldn't keep them lying about the place, could I?'

His own question did not require answering. Herr Hollmann went to the door and beckoned. A couple of policemen entered. One produced a pair of handcuffs, which he fitted over Conrad's wrists. The manacled carter sat staring down at the steel bands as though he couldn't believe what he saw.

'Take him away,' said the police chief, 'and then have this door put somewhere till it's needed.'

Conrad walked out of that office a changed man. He threw a final bitter glance at the door and made a sound like a muffled moan. The door was removed. The scraps of sealing wax and the original strands of horsehair were swept into an envelope, which was sealed and labelled and then put in the locked cabinet behind Herr Hollmann's desk. He sat down and began to make out his own report which would complete the Berlin police file on a man who would have to stand trial for mutiple murder.

While in prison awaiting trial Conrad's reason seemed to break down. He behaved like a madman and had to be put under restraint. He regained his lost control only hours before the trial, which did not last long, for there was almost no defence to be offered.

The jury found him guilty and he was sentenced to death. As he was removed from the court he looked an old man. One who had realized that he had gambled and lost – everything.

10 A PASSION
FOR SWEET PEAS

About fifty years ago a new couple came from Chicago to settle down in a pleasant bungalow a short distance outside the township of Aurora, in Illinois. The Lincolns had come there to enjoy retirement in an inviting rural area where life could be lived at a slower pace than in the busy city.

The husband, Warren Lincoln, was a middle-aged lawyer who had for years looked forward to occupying himself in a garden with no time or court-room pressures to invade his indulgence. His wife was physically a much more impressive person than her slightly built husband, and she had a brother, Byron Shoup, who had been described as a Mr Muscles, a large-framed man who indulged in physical exercise and muscle-building until it had become almost a way of life with him. Moreover, Byron had grown up from childhood with a strongly protective attitude towards his sister. Her marriage to Warren Lincoln had not changed this, and accordingly there was little love lost between the two males in Mrs Lincoln's life.

If coming to Aurora had provided her husband with hope that he would be freed from visits by his muscle-flexing brother-in-law he was to be bitterly disappointed. He was fifty and not in robust health, and his wife was an overbearing woman who openly bullied him. When brother and sister combined to offer a united front against him Warren Lincoln was a man reduced to slavish acquiescence to their wishes.

In Aurora his wife joined the local Women's Temperance Union and almost at once took a trenchant and personal line in debates that before her arrival had been easy-going arguments between friends. She introduced a sharp note of censure and acrimony into discussions, and became feared for her unguarded tongue. At home her husband was forbidden to seek any pleasure from smoking or an occasional glass of liquor and was ordered to accompany his domineering spouse to church on Sunday and to a regular Wednesday prayer meeting. Not surprisingly Warren Lincoln began to be pitied in the neighbourhood he had chosen for retirement.

Then Byron Shoup came from Nebraska for an extended stay with the Lincolns. He was given his own room and received the attentions from his sister that more rightfully could be expected by her neglected husband. Byron Shoup had the same bullying qualities of his sister developed to a more physically intimidating level.

He was the kind of man who took fierce pleasure in walking through his brother-in-law's sweet pea beds, trampling the fragile blooms under his broad feet, and then shouting with ribald laughter.

Exploiting his physical superiority in such ways over a man who could do no more than make a feeble protest gave Byron Shoup vast amusement, and he was encouraged to indulge his bullying by his sister, who, in turn, was able to find enjoyment in her husband's discomfiture.

Not long after Shoup arrived from Nebraska he took over Warren Lincoln's greenhouse and fitted it up as a gymnasium. It was the Prohibition Era of unhappy memory in the United States, and the brother had to keep his muscles in good trim for those raiding parties he joined under the aegis of the Women's Temperance Union.

The husband, who was kept outside these activities, discovered a way to obtain a secret revenge for the way he was being treated in his own home by this pair of Shoups. He eavesdropped when they discussed in unlowered voices the next speakeasy to be raided and put out of business. Surprisingly the raids became abortive, and for no reason understood by such action groups as the Women's Temperance Union. The raiding party would arrive and break down the door of a known or reported speakeasy and the raiders would be confronted by an empty apartment. A few such raids left them with rising claims for damage to property.

However, the popularity of Warren Lincoln in certain sections of the community rode high. For he had been the source of information about the raids that had enabled the speakeasy organizers to clear their premises. It seemed a huge joke that the seemingly inoffensive little man should be ruining his wife's plans and sending his burly brother-in-law on raids that became a costly waste of time. But after a number of such abortive raids had been made Mrs Lincoln, who was a shrewd and sharply intelligent woman where her own interests lay, became suspicious and set a trap. Her husband was caught eavesdropping.

'Byron,' she ordered her brother, 'you must deliver personal chastisement.'

Shoup was delighted to oblige. Robbed of the pleasure of breaking up the fittings and furniture in a speakeasy, he found keener satisfaction in sadistically beating up his weakling of a brother-in-law. The year 1921 ended with Byron Shoup still installed at the bungalow outside Aurora and Warren Lincoln's life a veritable purgatory. That Christmas was the most miserable he had ever lived. But the new year brought its promise of spring, and he again devoted himself to his passion for sweet peas. As the days grew lighter he worked longer hours in the garden. He grew so many sweet peas that something had to be done with them. The odd-job gardener named Frank who came to give him a hand with sticking the blooms suggested he market some. By mid-summer Warren Lincoln's sweet peas were bringing in a regular income, which was viewed with envy by Shoup, who told his sister, 'Lina, this money Warren's getting should go into your bank account.'

Mrs Lincoln thought about the suggestion and improved on it, as she considered. The money from the sale of sweet peas and other produce of her husband's garden should be put into a separate account at the bank. Then she was to be granted power of attorney over the balance. Warren Lincoln protested at what amounted to legal robbery, whereupon his wife sneeringly inquired if he wanted her brother to make him see sense.

Rather than take another beating at the ready fists of the sadistic bully the husband agreed to his wife's arrangement, but he neglected to inform her that he doubted whether she would enjoy the proceeds of such brutal coercion.

By the autumn the garden was looking bare, but he still spent long hours away from the bungalow. Another dreary Christmas left him feeling much happier, a state he was careful to conceal indoors. It was in January 1923 that he went into the town and visited one of the secret bars where he was a welcome stranger. He began a conversation with the barman that developed a personal note when he asked the man what he would do if he discovered his wife was receiving letters like the one Warren Lincoln showed him.

It was a typed letter, apparently sent from Chicago, and was signed simply 'George'. Whoever George was, he was writing in passionately explosive terms to Lina Lincoln. Instead of receiving advice from the barman Warren Lincoln was asked what he proposed to do. He appeared to reflect as he folded the letter and put it in his pocket and then claimed that it was her brother who had changed his wife, and he lamented that he hadn't turned both of them out of the house, as they deserved. He managed to express this opinion with a straight face, for he knew he had about as much chance of turning the Shoup brother and sister out of his bungalow as he had of starting his own speakeasy in it. But he also knew that when he left the bar, the barman, who had the garrulous readiness of his kind to impart scandal, would start a rumour circulating that would spread in ever-wider ripples.

Warren Lincoln arrived home to find his odd-job man tidying up in the greenhouse that had ceased to be a gymnasium from the moment the sweet pea money went into the new account. Frank and the man who employed him shared many things in common, including a bitter resentment of the bullying tactics of Byron Shoup and his sister's derisory comments about the garden.

Frank was the second man that day Warren Lincoln surprised with talk of throwing out the Shoups from his home.

'I'm going to do it, Frank, so don't try to dissuade me. There's only one thing I want you to do for me. If it comes to a fight, send for the police.'

It was a cold day, but Frank for once gave little mind to the January chill. He remained as close to the bungalow as he dared after Warren Lincoln had gone in. He waited for the fight he expected would break out. Instead, all he heard was Warren Lincoln's voice shaking with anger as he told his wife and her brother that they had finished running his life for him. Then he ordered them out of the house.

Outside, Frank waited for lightning to strike this hazardous challenge of authority. But again he was surprised when he heard Mrs Lincoln pleading with her husband to be allowed to stay. After the woman's voice he heard the brother's. Byron Shoup too was pleading. He even sounded scared, as though a turning worm had become a devouring python.

Warren Lincoln shouted accusations about George the letter-writer and the WTU, and how if the pair stayed he would ensure they could not face the scandal. After a time there was silence. The door opened and Warren Lincoln came out.

He saw Frank and said, ' I've done it. They're packing their bags right now, Frank. Tomorrow we'll be shut of them.'

Frank stared at his employer with kindling admiration for a strong man who could set his own house in order, then started for home. When he returned the next day it was to learn that Warren Lincoln had the bungalow to himself. The next time the retired lawyer appeared in his favourite speakeasy it was to be hailed as some sort of hero and to be clapped on the shoulders by frank admirers.

A short while later he asked the jobbing gardener, 'Seen any-one prowling around staring in the windows, Frank?'

The man looked at him, startled. 'Matter of fact,' he said, 'I did think I saw someone a couple of nights back.'

'Maybe I'd better have a word with the police,' Warren Lincoln told him. 'Can't take chances now I'm on my own.'

Frank Michels was the police chief in Aurora. He listened to what Warren Lincoln had to tell him with open surprise.

'Have you any idea who this prowler might be, Mr Lincoln?' he asked.

His surprise did not lessen when his visitor nodded and said, 'A private detective hired by my wife to recover these,' and handed over a pile of letters.

Frank Michels looked at the letters and saw that each was typed to Lina Lincoln in stridently affectionate terms and signed 'George'. The letters, he noted, had been posted in Chicago but not addressed to Aurora. They had been sent to Mrs Lincoln in care of a Chicago sub-post office. None of them held a return address. The visitor explained that he had found the letters concealed in a broom cupboard.

'What do you want from me?' Michels asked, frowning.

'Protection,' he was told. 'This prowler could be dangerous and I'm on my own since my wife left.'

The police chief pointed out that the number of men he had in Aurora was too limited for him to have any posted at the bungalow solely on the evidence of some letters. At this his visitor became angry and left.

There was no further news of the ex-lawyer or of the prowler and Michels forgot the visit. Three months passed, and then he received a forcible reminder when he was summoned to the bungalow by Frank the gardener, who sounded over the phone like a man who was in a panic. When Michels arrived at the bungalow it was to find the place ransacked. In the bedroom used by the owner there was blood on the bedclothes and on the wall.

There was no sign of Warren Lincoln. In the earth outside there were three sets of foot prints, which Michels concluded had been made by two men and a woman. A pair of Warren Lincoln's shoes showed that his feet were considerably smaller than either of the male prints. Michels was forced to believe that the prints had been made by Lina Lincoln and her brother Byron and some unknown man. Near to the road, not far from where the footprints ended on a hard surface, the Aurora police chief came upon a visiting card. On it was 'Milo Durand, Private Detective, Chicago, Illinois.' Remembering what Warren Lincoln had told him on his visit of some months back, Michels sought the gardener and asked him what he knew of a prowler or the disappearance of Warren Lincoln.

Frank could tell him little, but even that much suggested something had happened to Warren Lincoln. Michels phoned Chicago police headquarters and was told that no private eye named Milo Durand held a licence to operate in Chicago. A full-scale police hunt for the missing ex-lawyer was begun throughout the State. It ended when someone phoned Michels to tell him that Warren Lincoln was home working on his sweet peas. Michels drove to the bungalow to find the caller had told the truth, but the man tending his sweet peas was heavily bandaged and on visible parts of his flesh were discolorations like deep bruising.

Warren Lincoln explained that he had escaped after being beaten up and taken away by Shoup and a stranger who had accompanied his wife when she came to collect the letters she had hidden. He had been taken to Cleveland, Ohio, and kept prisoner in a room with no window, where he lost count of time and the days that passed. His chance to escape came one night when the man who was his guard became drunk and fell into a heavy stupor.

'Did she get the letters?' Michels asked.

'No,' said the bandaged man. 'They're in a safe deposit box in Chicago.'

'Get them out,' Michels told him. 'They may hold a clue I can work on.'

But this time Warren Lincoln showed a reluctance to produce the letters, pleading that he had been through enough and now wanted to be left alone to raise his sweet peas. The police chief took his departure feeling frustrated at the outcome of his visit. He couldn't reconcile this change in Warren Lincoln with the man's behaviour of three months earlier.

He started an investigation that received no publicity in Aurora. From the Women's Temperance Union he obtained samples of Lina Lincoln's handwriting, and from the Chicago sub-post office where the letters signed 'George' had been delivered he obtained samples of the writing allegedly made by Mrs Lincoln in an application for their *poste restante* service. The two samples of writing were very different.

The bank where Warren Lincoln had a safe deposit box was found, upon inquiry, to be not very far from the sub-post office. Michels interviewed its manager and was informed Warren Lincoln had no account, only a rented deposit box. A fresh inquiry was started among small printers, and he found the firm that had printed the Milo Durand card. The date of the order was a month before the Shoups vacated the bungalow. The man who had taken the order had a clear recollection of the person who had given it.

'He was a little guy,' he told Michels, 'who told me he was playing a joke on someone.'

Asked to describe this small customer, he gave Michels a recognizable description of Warren Lincoln.

The Aurora police chief knew he had to take his inquiry further. He went to Chicago police headquarters and talked to several detectives who had known the lawyer before his retirement of a couple of years before. He was told a startling but illuminating fact. Warren Lincoln could imitate other people's voices and he had acquired a court-room habit of intimidating witnesses by using their voices when he examined them in an attempt to discredit their testimony.

Frank Michels knew then that the gardener Frank had not heard the voices of Lina Lincoln and Byron Shoup on the night his employer had alerted him to call the police if there was a fight. He had heard Warren Lincoln imitating their voices. The next day when he arrived at the bungalow the brother and sister were gone, according to Warren Lincoln. So Frank had not seen them at the time his master delivered his ultimatum or subsequently.

Michels again drove out to the bungalow and there was Warren Lincoln again working in his sweet pea beds, tending the pastel-tinted blooms with soft-handed care. Not far away, in front of the bungalow, were two large flower boxes. Both had been freshly painted.

Michels stood glancing around the garden with interest, unperceived for some time by the man whose undivided attention was given to his sweet peas.

When at length Warren Lincoln turned the police chief saw he had discarded his bandages. The ex-lawyer smiled invitingly.

'Look nice, don't they?' he said nodding to the blooms he had been tending.

'Very nice,' nodded Michels, and turned to the brightly painted flower boxes. 'New, aren't they?' he asked.

'Yes,' Warren Lincoln said, smiling as though pleased that the police chief had observed the fresh addition to his garden. 'I thought they'd brighten up the front of the bungalow.'

Michels walked towards the boxes, saw that the soil in them was smoothed over.

'What have you sown in them?' he inquired.

'Sweet peas. You know, I can't seem to get enough of them. They should be looking pretty when I get back, Mr Michels.'

The police chief registered surprise. 'You're not leaving Aurora?'

'Only for a short vacation. That's all. I feel in need of one and I'd sooner take it now rather than later.'

The two men chatted about the garden for a short while longer before Michels drove away. The police chief knew he had arrived at a crossroads in his own career. What he did next would affect what he would be able to do in the immediate future, and upon that depended whether he made a bad mistake or achieved a signal triumph as a detective.

He knew that Warren Lincoln, the man who had made a name for himself harassing witnesses in trials that had made headlines throughout the Middle West, had only minutes before been trying to conceal his contempt for the man he considered a backwater cop with a fancy title. But he had once penetrated the ex-lawyer's complacency. That had been upon the occasion of Warren Lincoln's first meeting with him, when he had come to ask for protection. By refusing to comply he had rattled his visitor badly, who had not been clever enough to cover up his violent reaction to being crossed. This had been sufficient to show that there were secret depths to Warren Lincoln. He was capable of planning in anticipation of achieving a desired result, but if his plans were upset he could be brought close to panic.

He sat in his car thinking about what could really have happened in the bungalow before Frank the gardener heard those voices. One thing was very sure. Neither the sister nor her brother had been in a position to protest at the charade Warren Lincoln had carried through for his audience of one behind a closed door.

A few days later the bungalow was closed and Warren Lincoln went for his holiday. As soon as Frank Michels learned this he sought out the gardener Frank. He needed to be very sure of what the man had seen and heard on that night when Warren Lincoln again became master in his own house.

At first Frank was suspicious of the police chief and the reason for his call and the questions put to him, but Michels told him he had to get things straightened out for the record and it was unfortunate that Warren Lincoln was away, otherwise he could have cleared up this business without having to bother Frank. His suspicions allayed, Frank talked freely and with no sign of having inhibitions on the subject of the Shoups, whom he criticized and condemned for their treatment not only of Warren Lincoln, but himself.

Slowly the police chief worked his way round to the night that was important to the case he had been building for weeks. Everything depended on what Frank told him now, at a moment when the gardener felt free to tell the truth without restraint. He learned, as he had surmised, that the gardener waiting outside in the January cold had only heard the voices of Mrs Lincoln and her brother talking to Warren Lincoln. He had not seen them or even heard their movements inside the bungalow. He had, in actual fact, not seen them since earlier that day. Certainly not after his employer had told him he was going into the bungalow to give the pair an ultimatum that would result in their leaving without delay.

'They were gone when you arrived next morning, Frank?'

'Yes. Mr Lincoln told me they were packing their bags that night even before I left.'

Frank seemed amused by the victory his employer had won with his threat about showing the letters to the WTU.

Michels became casual in his manner, talking about Warren Lincoln's activities besides gardening. When Frank informed him that his employer had a typewriter the police chief felt excited, but almost in the next breath the gardener added that the typewriter had been sold some weeks before. When Michels left the gardener had no idea that he had helped Frank Michels to come to the most momentous decision in his career.

It took time and plodding inquiry, but Michels succeeded in finding the dealer who had bought Warren Lincoln's typewriter. The man still had the machine. The police chief procured a warrant to search the deposit box in the Chicago bank. In it, as he had been told, were the letters ostensibly sent by 'George'. They had all been typed on a machine with a defective 'e'.

The typewriter Warren Lincoln had sold after his wife's disappearance with her brother had a similarly defective 'e', and

Michels knew an expert would pronounce that the 'George' letters had been typed on that machine.

Frank Michels had his case. He waited until Warren Lincoln returned from his vacation. Then he went out to the bungalow with a couple of his men. This time he felt very sure that he could spare them to visit the Lincoln home. The three Aurora police found the man they had come for working among his sweet peas. For a moment Frank Michels felt he couldn't credit that the man tending his flowers could have done what he knew he had. Nothing could have seemed more remote from those beds of fragile blooms than murderous violence.

But when Warren Lincoln turned and saw him there was no welcoming smile nor hint of contempt for a country cop with a fancy title. It was as though he had an instinctive awareness of the reason for the visit. But this time there was no sign of panic. Perhaps the holiday away from Aurora had steadied the man's nerves, Michels thought.

He said, 'I'm arresting you for the murder of your wife and your brother-in-law. You imitated their voices and I've evidence that was something you could very well do.'

'You'll have to prove your words,' the ex-lawyer reminded him.

'I'll do that.'

Warren Lincoln glanced at the men accompanying the police chief. 'Send them out of earshot and I'll tell you something,' he smiled, but there was no warmth in the smile.

Michels glanced at his men and they walked away.

The man who had a passion for sweet peas said in a conversational tone, 'You're right, of course, Mr Michels. I destroyed the bodies in the greenhouse furnace, but that's only my word, and even I can't prove it.' His smile came back. 'Their heads are in those flower boxes – I buried them in quicklime. A nice touch, don't you think?'

'I'll turn out the boxes,' Michels said dourly.

'A waste of time. As you can see, I planted the boxes with sweet peas, as I told you. I've kept them well watered, which helped the quicklime to work fast. Whatever's in those boxes will be unrecognizable.'

But the man of law who had planned so secretly and cleverly

was wrong in his final and most important claim to success. Michels had the flower boxes turned out and he found the heads, both of which were still recognizable, for the gardener Frank had been guilty of a silly yet very common error. Instead of buying quicklime, as instructed, he had returned with slaked lime. Whereas the quicklime would quickly have destroyed the grisly contents of the flower boxes, the slaked lime preserved them.

The trial of Warren Lincoln created a sensation throughout the Middle West of that time, for the work undertaken by the country police chief warranted large headlines. It also earned the grim verdict of 'Guilty' passed by the jury. The prisoner was sentenced to prison for life and was taken to the penitentiary at Joliet, where he died in 1941, a man for whom sweet peas were only a bitter memory.

11 THE CAPTAIN
WHO LIKED CATS

When Alphonse Bertillon, the famous French criminologist, received a visit from a friend of long standing he was surprised to learn that Maître Hoffmayer's call was not a purely social one. A good many years had passed since Bertillon had met his future wife by chance[1] and the criminologist was now at the peak of his career, a man consulted by police chiefs from all over Europe and even from the United States and one who had acquired many friends and also a number of enemies.

His visitor was taken into Bertillon's study. Outside its window the plane-trees were in leaf and daylight shone on the bindings of the library Bertillon had inherited from his father.

The lawyer said, 'What I have to tell you, Alphonse, will convince you that Captain Larsen was murdered. But only you will be able to prove it.'

Hoffmayer began a story about a Swedish sea-captain named Larsen, who rather late in life by French standards had married a woman he met in Paris and not long afterwards gave up the sea and retired. During his career at sea he had earned good wages and, being a frugal man, had saved most of them, so that when he ceased being a bachelor he was a man of substance, able to afford a pleasant home in a good residential suburb of the French capital. The house had a large garden and was secluded. Captain Larsen seemed a man blessed by fortune and his friends envied him.

However, the sea-captain had a brother. This was Dr Larsen, a man of medicine, who had felt the same call of the sea in his

---

[1] See 'They Met in the Rush Hour' in the author's *Famous Stories of Scientific Detection* (Arthur Barker Ltd).

youth. Accordingly, his examinations passed, he did not seek a practice in some Swedish town, but secured a post as a ship's doctor.

Both Larsens, in their different ways, were seafaring men.

However, what seemed to be a curious coincidence was the doctor's retiring from the sea almost at the same time as the sea-captain. But even more curious was the place the doctor chose for his retirement. He had found a modest bungalow suitable for a bachelor like himself not far from the sea-captain's home in the southern suburb of Bicêtre.

'It is actually at the far end of the very extensive grounds of Captain Larsen's home,' the lawyer explained to Bertillon. 'But the two brothers, you understand, have kept their own separate establishments.'

'One of them has been murdered,' Bertillon reminded his guest, 'the sea-captain. How?'

'Of tetanus.'

The criminologist made no attempt to conceal his surprise at this news. Tetanus is more commonly termed lockjaw. To die from it was not precisely a rare hazard, but to be murdered by tetanus was something unknown. Bertillon could not conceal the doubt that came to his mind.

'I know what you're thinking, Alphonse,' said the lawyer. 'But I've come only after being very sure of my facts.'

He continued with his story of how, while they were at sea, the Larsen brothers had each made a will naming the other as sole heir. Making such wills had been a simple family precaution by men who faced dangers unfamiliar to those who lived their lives ashore. The wills had been drawn up and signed years before, and for a long time neither had seen any cause to alter the arrangement. Both were unmarried. Their parents were dead. Each was his brother's next of kin.

However, not long after he had settled down in his new home with a wife the captain had remembered his will and come to the conclusion that, now he had the responsibility of providing for his wife, he should alter the terms of his will to benefit her.

He had gone to a lawyer and discussed the matter. The solicitor had advised making a new will to avoid complications.

In the new will Madame Larsen was named as joint heir with the doctor.

Alphonse Bertillon had always been a man who could jump to a conclusion without having to retrace his steps.

He demonstrated as much that day to Maître Hoffmayer when he broke in abruptly to say, 'So you're here on behalf of the widow, my friend.'

The lawyer shrugged expressively. 'But of course.'

'Does the captain's widow believe the doctor killed his brother in order to inherit his share of the dead man's estate?' Bertillon inquired.

The lawyer shook his head.

'No,' he said and paused to lean forward. 'But I do.'

He went on to inform the criminologist that he had made inquiries and learned that, since taking up residence in the bungalow, the doctor had secured a position with a local hospital. But very recently he had been discharged. The lawyer had found it difficult to get anyone to talk about a scandal that had been hushed up, but one man had told him in confidence that Dr Larsen had been summarily dismissed by the director of the hospital after some corpses in the hospital mortuary had been found with what were believed to be cabalistic signs marked on their forehead.

'You mean there's been talk of witchcraft?' Bertillon asked. 'This doctor seems to be a rather unusual character, following his brother to sea and then into retirement – only he doesn't retire, he becomes involved with suggested black magic and tetanus. Don't you think it sounds a little far-fetched, my friend?'

The visitor lifted his hands and let them fall in his lap.

'Just what anyone would think, I agree. But I believe this is a case that you and your colleagues in the Sûreté should investigate. To my mind there is definitely more than a suspicion of murder.'

Bertillon sat thinking about what he had heard. 'You haven't told Madame Larsen of your intention to visit me?'

'Naturally not,' the lawyer replied. 'The poor woman has been quite overcome with shock.'

Before Maître Hoffmayer left Bertillon had agreed to make

inquiries of his own. 'But don't expect much,' he warned the lawyer. 'I never believe murder has been done until I find proof. Anything less than absolute proof is at best mere theory, and at worst sheer guesswork.'

Bertillon was not a man to waste time when he considered haste essential. When he arrived at the Larsen home in Bicêtre, accompanied by two Sûreté detectives, he had already made inquiries at the Lariboisière Hospital, only to be confronted by a wall of professional silence. This had intrigued him. The director, when pressed, had admitted that Dr Jarg Larsen had been dismissed from the regular staff for infringing hospital rules, but he insisted the dismissal was merely a matter of internal discipline.

However, Bertillon was a man with many contacts in the French capital. From a very different quarter he was informed that some scandal at the hospital had been kept from public notice by Dr Larsen's dismissal and a severe lecture on the value of loyalty and silence that had been delivered to the remaining staff members by an agitated director. It sounded very mysterious, but Bertillon, although intrigued, still kept an open mind.

He found Madame Larsen to be an attractive woman in early middle age. He judged her to be emotional and probably mercurial in temperament, qualities that could have made her attractive in the eyes of a somewhat staid Swedish sea-captain. When Bertillon called on her he found she had company. Her cousin, Mademoiselle Bigoud, had come to stay with her and help her to recover from the shock of her husband's sudden demise. But the criminologist was surprised when he learned that this first explanation of Mademoiselle Bigoud's presence was not what he had been led to believe was the truth. Mademoiselle Bigoud was certainly acting as companion to her cousin the new widow, but she had been staying in the house from a few days after the wedding.

Bertillon found Mademoiselle Bigoud more difficult to assess than her emotional cousin. She had depths of character and although she appeared ready to talk, she seemed only to talk about things she wished to impart. Her reticence was calculated, just as much as any confidence she shared.

It was Mademoiselle Bigoud who told Bertillon, when her cousin was not present, of a quarrel between the Larsen brothers. This quarrel, which had been explosive and bitter, occurred just a few days before the captain was attacked by a strange paralysis that left him unable to speak.

Beyond this Mademoiselle Bigoud would not commit her cautious self.

When questioned about the quarrel the widow began a rambling tirade that was not very coherent. Bertillon decided it would be best to postpone questioning her. He interviewed the doctor who signed the death certificate, and was informed that the man had been summoned shortly after daylight and arrived to find the captain in a coma.

'His jaws were locked in the familiar rictus of tetanus, Monsieur Bertillon,' the doctor confirmed, 'with the distinctive arching of the body.'

The doctor showed surprise when Bertillon asked him to visit the mortuary, but raised no objection. With the medical man looking on the criminologist examined the flesh of the corpse under a magnifying glass. He stopped when the glass was over the right leg and pointed to some faint scratches.

'Did you note these, doctor?' Bertillon asked.

'Monsieur, they are only scratches.' The doctor shrugged.

Bertillon was given the dead man's trousers. The right leg had some snagged threads corresponding with the position of the scratches over the knee. The doctor was shaking his head, puzzled, and was glad when Bertillon told him they had finished their examination. To the doctor it had been an officious waste of time. However, Bertillon's detective interest deepened when he learned that the suit with the snagged threads in the trousers was one Larsen had worn the day before he was taken ill. The person who told him this was Mademoiselle Bigoud.

'I am very sure, monsieur,' she said with an air of conviction. 'I remember the captain snatching the cat away from his brother. He sat with it on his lap and its claws dug into his suit when it scrambled to get away.'

Bertillon said he had looked for a cat but without seeing one in the house.

'It was the blue Persian,' Mademoiselle Bigoud explained.

This was one of the doctor's cats. He kept several in his bungalow.

Bertillon had missed Dr Larsen each time he had arrived at the small estate in Bicêtre. The Swedish doctor was away from home, he was told. Bertillon went to the Lariboisière Hospital and spoke to one of Dr Larsen's former colleagues. This man surprised Bertillon by venting the frank opinion that the Swede was insane.

'How do you mean?' Bertillon inquired.

'He's very eccentric and I know he dabbles in the occult.'

The hospital doctor explained that he believed Dr Larsen's interest in occult matters was responsible for strange marks being scratched on the foreheads of patients that had died.

'I don't understand it, and this is only my personal opinion, you understand.'

'I understand,' Bertillon assured the uncomfortable doctor. 'I shall see that no scandal attaches to the hospital.'

He made a third visit to Bicêtre with two Sûreté detectives, this time expressly to see Dr Larsen. His knock at the door produced no answer. Either the doctor remained away from home or he was avoiding the criminologist. This time, however, Bertillon had come prepared to ensure that his visit was not wasted. He nodded to one of the Sûreté men, who produced some skeleton keys and with one of them opened the door.

Bertillon had been told that the Swedish doctor had a laboratory at the rear of his bungalow. He went straight to it, entered, and pulled up in surprise.

From a low ceiling hung a stuffed crocodile. It was covered with a layer of grey dust. Stuffed birds and fish in glass cases decorated the dark walls, one of which held a bookcase with many medical volumes and also some worn books on alchemy and the practices of the medieval alchemists. Several titles dealt with necromancy. These were the books without dust on their tops.

A scrabbling of claws against metal turned Bertillon's attention to a steel cage containing a number of cats of different breeds. They looked sleepy and one was a blue Persian.

The criminologist walked around this makeshift laboratory aware of the warring smells he could distinguish. The cat smell was unpleasant, but there was also a strong reek of disinfectant. He asked the Sûreté men what they thought it was. One said readily it was carbolic and the other agreed. The first suggested the cats might have a disease.

Bertillon looked for possible signs of the absent Dr Larsen holding an interest in vivisection. He found none and moved to the cage of cats. He unlatched the door, reached for the blue Persian, and lifted the animal out. At once he became aware of an even stronger reek of disinfectant. It came from the cat's front paws.

He put the animal on the floor and it rubbed against his legs, purring.

'Take a look at this, monsieur,' said one of the Sûreté detectives.

Bertillon returned the cat to the cage and crossed to the man who had spoken. He was standing by a writing desk that had been pushed into the angle of two walls and turning over a pale object in his hands. He gave it to Bertillon.

The object was a long-handled piece of carved ivory, quite slender, and one end was shaped like a claw.

'It was in the pen tray,' said the Sûreté man.

Several pens and pencils lay in the tray beside a corroded bottle of ink. Bertillon and his strong lens moved over the desk top and the floor near the desk's legs. Tiny scrapings of ivory were found on the floor, where they had been brushed from the desk. He decided that the slender strip of ivory had been scraped to a claw. He sniffed it. The claw was odourless and Bertillon put it back in the tray.

He turned to the missing doctor's microscope, which one of the Sûreté men had uncovered. A slide was set in position, and when Bertillon peered at what the slide held he recognized tetanus bacilli. There could be a number of innocent explanations for such a slide, as Bertillon was well aware. But there could be one that was far from innocent.

When he left Bicêtre the two Sûreté detectives remained to watch the dead captain's house and the bungalow of the absent doctor. Later that night Mademoiselle Bigoud summoned the doctor who had attended the dying captain. He arrived to find the widow dying of the same horrible disease – tetanus. He notified the police. Bertillon arrived shortly after the distressed doctor had covered Madame Larsen's distorted features. He examined the dead woman, stared around the death chamber, and went down on his hands and knees beside the bed. From the floor he picked up an indelible pencil, for which he had been looking after observing a tiny purple stain on the tip of the dead woman's tongue.

He had also found a faint scratch on an upper arm.

When he left the room where Madame Larsen lay the criminologist sought Mademoiselle Bigoud.

'Did your cousin hold a cat in her arms recently?' he asked.

The question surprised her, but she said, 'Yes. Like the captain, she loved cats.'

When Bertillon returned to Dr Larsen's bungalow the owner was still absent. His Sûreté assistant opened the door for him, and he went through to the laboratory to be met with a stronger smell of disinfectant. He traced it to the front paws of one of the caged cats.

The cat was a sleepy tortoiseshell.

The smell on the paws of the blue Persian had almost gone. On the other hand, the ivory claw had disappeared from the pen tray.

He crossed the garden to the house. Mademoiselle Bigoud seemed to be expecting him.

'Was it the blue Persian your cousin held?' he inquired.

The woman shook her head. 'No, the tortoiseshell.'

'Dr Larsen was here?'

'Only for a few minutes. He took the cat away.'

Dr Larsen must have been very careful in his movements, for he had not been seen by the Sûreté man posted to watch the bungalow. Bertillon had more men set to watch the grounds, and this time when the elusive Jarg Larsen returned to his bungalow he was observed darting between high shrubs and bushes to a back door screened by a tree.

When Bertillon made an unexpected appearance at a late hour the Swedish doctor was obviously taken by surprise and flustered.

'What do you want, Monsieur Bertillon?' he asked, his manner openly hostile.

'To show you something, monsieur.'

The criminologist produced a search warrant and called two Sûreté men from the grounds.

'You know what to look for,' he told them.

They went through the bungalow, including the laboratory, without finding what Bertillon sought. When they reported the criminologist nodded. 'Then it is most likely in one of his pockets,' he said. 'Search Dr Larsen.'

The search was begun over the doctor's violent protest, but it did not last long. The dead captain's will was found in his brother's inside pocket. When Bertillon unfolded it he saw a wide smudge in one margin.

In his own laboratory at police headquarters Bertillon treated the will to an iodine vapour test, which brought up well-nigh erased indentations made by indelible pencil. The brown vapour tracings were photographed and the result enlarged. Bertillon read what Madame Larsen had written shortly before her death in the margin of her dead husband's will. The words had been written where the large smudge had been treated.

The message ran :

'I die like my husband. The cats' claws carry the disease that is death, and I accuse my husband's brother of our murders. I write this on the will because I know he dare not destroy it.'

Bertillon appreciated the dying woman's shrewdness as expressed in the last sentence. She had provided the authorities with an accuser as well as a motive. He went back to Bicêtre to have Jarg Larsen formally arrested, but was too late to stop a desperate man from giving way to his despair.

The bungalow door was wide when he arrived. Inside was the body of a Sûreté detective. A severe blow from behind had smashed the man's skull. The weapon lay nearby. It was a broad strip of iron, one end still tacky with drying blood. The dead detective's colleague was missing.

This time, when Bertillon arrived at the house, Mademoiselle Bigoud could tell him nothing new. She too was dead. It looked like suicide at first, but a smell of bitter almonds still clung to the drinking glass that had been rinsed. When the body was moved the missing ivory claw was found. She had been lying on it. On its tip was a red stain.

Bertillon phoned police headquarters. A hunt for Dr Jarg Larsen was organized.

In those days before the First World War such a business could take a long time. There were few short cuts. There were no radio stations, no police aircraft or helicopters, and an inquiry could not be internationally handled by Interpol. If one was temperamentally impatient one went through a bad time. Fortunately for Alphonse Bertillon, he had more patience than most men.

On the second day after he had given the French police the alert the missing Sûreté man phoned from Belgium. He reported that he had followed Dr Larsen when the man rushed from the bungalow with a suitcase, obviously in flight. He had been given no chance earlier to make a direct report.

The man was informed that the doctor was now wanted for murder and the Belgian police had been informed. He was instructed to make himself known to them and get the Belgians to arrest Larsen. After the necessary formalities had been completed he was to bring the prisoner to Paris.

When eventually Jarg Larsen stepped from a train at the Gare de l'Est, in the custody of the Sûreté man and two Belgian detectives it was to find a reception committee awaiting him. He stared at only one face among the others. To Jarg Larsen the face of Alphonse Bertillon was like the face of doom.

Bertillon's face was suddenly frowning. The criminologist pushed though the escort of detectives. His voice was sharp with concern when he said, 'Dr Larsen, you're ill.'

The prisoner's mouth twisted. 'I'm dying,' he confided and tried to smile, but it was a forlorn attempt for his throat was constricted by pain-wrenched neck muscles, and his words were barely audible.

Dr Larsen was not taken to police headquarters. He was hurried by cab to hospital. When the man, now near to collapse, was undressed Bertillon saw the red scratch mark on his neck. He handed the heavily breathing man a mirror. Larsen stared at the red mark under his jaw.

'The ivory claw?' Bertillon inquired.

The man in the hospital bed nodded and let the mirror fall on the covers.

'Mademoiselle Bigoud?' A second nod. 'When you gave her the drink with prussic acid and she realized what you had done?' A third nod. 'So she was prepared for you?'

There were no further nods. Jarg Larsen opened his mouth and gasped as though fighting for air. He and Bertillon were sharing a secret both men understood as they watched each other. Had the doctor not tried to escape, but remained in Paris, he just might have saved his life if he had received instant treatment. But he would have been saving it for Monsieur de Paris, as Parisians dubbed the city's executioner who operated the guillotine's axe. By flight, the doctor had chosen the more speedy but more painful death, without facing two years of legal wrangling that his lawyers could not win for him. It had been the choice of a gambler who had failed.

When Bertillon left the hospital Larsen was unconscious. The criminologist took with him the black suitcase that had accompanied the doctor on his futile flight. Inside was a writing pad with an account of what had happened written on the top pages, presumably on the journey to Belgium. Bertillon read that his taking the will had decided the doctor he had to get away, but he could not leave Mademoiselle Bigoud to talk. He had not missed the ivory claw because, after first deciding to use it, he had changed his mind and used the cats since his brother and sister-in-law had been fond of them. But Mademoiselle Bigoud was suspicious, and he could not rely on the cats for a third time. So he called for a talk and a drink, and when she knew how he had tricked her she had produced the ivory claw and in the struggle managed to scratch his neck. At the bottom of his account of how Fate and his own greed had destroyed four lives he had written as a sort of postscript: 'My brother should never have left the sea. Nor should I. It was our salvation.'

What was the meaning of the last words Bertillon never discovered, even when he went through all the papers the Larsen brothers had left in Bicêtre.

In the afternoon of the day following Jarg Larsen's return to Paris the hospital telephoned to announce that their patient was dead.

'We would like the police to remove the body,' the caller said, 'as we understand it officially remains in their custody and we require the bed.'

Hardly an epitaph, but perhaps they were the kindest words that could be said of Dr Jarg Larsen at that time. They promised that he could be forgotten.

Except in the records of the Sûreté Nationale and the private files of Alphonse Bertillon.

12 THE OTHER CARTRIDGE CASE

Number 45 Chester Square is a Georgian residence in London's Belgravia. In the summer of 1946 King George of the Hellenes decided to lease it as his residence while awaiting a recall to Athens to resume his reign as monarch of Greece. The Second World War had been over in Europe for more than a year when His Majesty made a Sunday visit to Chester Square to see for himself how a number of approved alterations had been carried out.

However, bottles of milk on the doorstep at three o'clock in the afternoon were not objects to encourage the royal anticipation of what would be found. The Greek King's bewilderment and annoyance increased when he entered number 45. His housekeeper, Miss Elizabeth McLindon, was apparently not there to receive him, and some of the rooms on the ground floor were locked. The keys for those locked rooms could not be found by the mystified attendants accompanying His Majesty.

After wandering through the rooms that were not locked the royal party left. In no sense could it be called a successful or encouraging visit to what was about to become a royal residence. The date was 9 June 1946.

A few days later, when it was found that the doors on the ground floor remained locked and there was still no sign of Miss McLindon, the police were informed. The locked doors were forced open.

In one room was the body of Elizabeth McLindon. It was slumped forward in a chair. She had been shot from behind, and whoever had fired the weapon must have been well known to the housekeeper. The police surgeon who examined the body announced that death had occurred on the Saturday before the Greek King's visit. That would be 8 June. At the time of the examination she had been dead a week.

The one immediate clue discovered by the police who broke into the room and found the body was a cartridge case of thirty-two calibre. It had dropped on the floor not far from the chair in which the victim sat. The police traced the bullet's trajectory in a line with the wall at which the dead woman had appeared to be staring. They dug a spent thirty-two bullet out of its plaster.

When a conference was held at Scotland Yard it was agreed that two high-ranking officers should head the investigation. So the Yard team that worked on the case was directed after the first few hours by Deputy Commander William Rawlings and Superintendent James Ball. They sought details about the dead woman, and learned that she was forty-one years old and had been engaged as housekeeper on 26 April after references from a number of highly respectable employers had been considered. The dead woman, from what the police could discover, had been a very suitable housekeeper.

But apparently she had been a woman with a secret. She had not been murdered by a chance intruder. The first clue that offered a line of inquiry was provided by a letter addressed to the dead woman. It had been delivered by post and remained unopened when the police found it. The letter had been written in Brighton by someone who signed himself as 'Arthur', who had become anxious because there was no reply to his phone calls. He wanted reassurance from the housekeeper that nothing had happened to her.

The writer of the letter was identified by the dead woman's sister as Arthur Robert Boyce.

'He is my sister's fiancé,' she explained. 'Arthur and Elizabeth only became engaged recently.'

But inquiry proved that something significant had happened on the Saturday Miss McLindon was murdered. It was the day bombers flew over London in a victory formation to mark the first anniversary of peace after the recent destructive war. Faces at the windows of neighbouring Georgian houses saw the housekeeper come out of number 45, apparently in a hurry, and hasten away. Not long afterwards Arthur Boyce had arrived at number

45 and after ringing the bell without gaining admittance pummelled on the front door. When it became plain that no one was going to answer his summons he too left, in the same direction as his fiancée.

Superintendent Ball went to Brighton and arrived at Boyce's lodging when he was out. The Yard man questioned the landlady, and she confirmed that for some days past her lodger had seemed anxious about where his fiancée was. On the 11th he had gone to London but had returned without seeing her and told his landlady, 'The King must have gone off to one of his other places and taken her with him.'

Later, after Boyce had learned that his fiancée had been found murdered, he had appeared to break down. He displayed considerable emotion when Ball questioned him. He kept brushing back his untidy hair with a hand and blinking at Ball from behind large round spectacles. He told the Yard man that he had last seen his fiancée on the evening of the 8th. Afterwards he had written because he had phoned repeatedly without getting any reply at the Chester Square number. Because he couldn't understand this continued silence he had phoned Elizabeth's sister in Liverpool and asked if she knew where Elizabeth had gone.

Ball widened the scope of his questions. He wanted to know if Arthur Boyce's fiancée had had any other men friends. The reply was given without hesitation. Two. One of them was a violent man who could conceivably have taken revenge on the dead housekeeper. After this statement Boyce leaned forward as though to impress a point on his listener.

'It could have been an assassin,' he said.

When Ball asked what he meant he said someone might have broken into the Chester Square house intending to assassinate the King. Finding the King not in residence, and fearing that he would be recognized if he left without killing the housekeeper, the intruder had shot Elizabeth McLindon.

'What makes you think a would-be assassin would call at Chester Square?' Ball asked.

'All kinds of curious people called at the house,' he was informed. 'Elizabeth told me.'

Ball wasn't convinced. He thought he had detected an irrational quality in Arthur Boyce, who was employed at that time as a painter on Brighton's Palace Pier. After telling Boyce that the man had been helpful the Yard man left and walked to a phone kiosk, from which he rang the Yard and was switched through to the Criminal Records Office. When he left the phone kiosk he continued to the Palace Pier and talked to some of the men still working on it. One of them recalled seeing Boyce pull an automatic from his pocket.

'Don't wave that thing about unless it's not loaded,' he had told Boyce.

'Oh, it's loaded all right,' Boyce had boasted. 'There are five up the spout.'

After leaving the pier Ball rang the Yard again. The CRO was able to give him the information he had requested earlier. Boyce had a record of serving eighteen months for bigamy. At that moment there was a notice out for him. He was wanted to answer certain charges involving a number of fraudulent cheques. One of these bore the name Papanikolaou, which was the name of the Greek King's private secretary.

Ball had sufficient evidence to warrant taking Arthur Boyce to London, but what he had pointed only to opportunity and possibility. He had not discovered anything that might be called a reasonable motive for the crime, and he had not found anything so far that directly pointed at Boyce as being implicated in the shooting.

If he found the murder weapon, of course, that would close the case.

He returned to Boyce's lodgings and another round of questions and a search. There were few personal possessions in Boyce's room, and the man seemed to live very frugally. His job as a painter on the pier did not allow him to live in luxury, and searching his apartment was no complicated task.

But one thing that interested the superintendent when he saw it was an old luggage label. It was one Boyce had made out for himself some time before, and on it he gave as his address that of a John Rowland in Caernarvon. To the somewhat frustrated detective it seemed that a journey to Caernarvon seemed too many steps in the wrong direction, but if he failed to find anything offering a better lead he knew he would be going to Wales.

He arrested Boyce for passing bogus cheques and took his prisoner back to London to be formally charged. Then Ball had a conference with Rawlings. Both experienced Yard men agreed that the case against Boyce looked promising enough, but it had yet to be proved in a way that would please the Director of Public Prosecutions. This would entail securing additional evidence that would make the case watertight.

'You'd better see what you can dig up in Caernarvon, John,' Rawlings told the man who had just returned from Brighton. 'It's a long shot, but the long shot occasionally comes up.'

'Let's hope it does this time,' Ball grinned.

A few hours later he had little hope that it would. He had arrived in the Welsh town where traditionally the Prince of Wales has his inauguration in conditions of medieval splendour and gone to interview John Rowland only to learn that the man he wished to speak to had left the town.

'Do you know where I can find him?' Ball inquired of a person who had known Rowland well.

'He's somewhere in the Army,' was the not very helpful reply.

The journey to Wales had been wasted effort and the long shot had not come off.

However, Ball did not stop trying to find the man who might have valuable information to give him. He returned to London and approached the War Office. It took time, but after a good deal of checking and inquiry Rowland was located, and again Superintendent John Ball took up his travels.

Rowland proved to be helpful. He readily admitted that for a time he had shared rooms with Arthur Boyce. He went on to explain that during the period they lodged together he had bought a Browning automatic.

'It was obtained quite legally,' he assured Ball. 'I wasn't doing anything I shouldn't by buying the gun.'

Ball accepted this assurance.

'What was the calibre?' he asked.

'A thirty-two.'

One important part of the case seemed to be closing satisfactorily.

'Boyce knew you had the gun, I suppose?' Ball continued.

Rowland nodded. 'He not only knew it, he wanted it. He offered to buy it from me.'

'But you didn't sell it to him?'

'No. I saw no reason why I should.'

'Where is the gun now?'

That was the question that caused John Rowland to hesitate. He looked at the Yard man uncertainly.

'I don't know,' he said with his same air of being open and candid. 'But I suspect Boyce took it.'

'Tell me what makes you suspect that,' Ball invited the other man.

Rowland told the Yard detective that several times Boyce had asked the man sharing his lodging to change his mind about selling him the gun, but Rowland had not changed his mind. After a time the subject of the Browning had been dropped and neither of the men made any further reference to it. Some months passed, and one day after Boyce had left the lodging and Rowland was packing his bags for a return to Wales he found his Browning automatic was missing.

'I searched everywhere but didn't find it,' he told Ball. 'It seemed obvious what had happened. Arthur Boyce had taken it and said nothing.'

'Did you do anything?' Ball inquired.

'I certainly did,' said Rowland. 'I had his address and I wrote him a rough note telling him to return the gun. He didn't even reply.'

By this time John Ball had little doubt that the gun that had fired the fatal bullet in 45 Chester Square was John Rowland's. But knowledge was not proof. Accordingly he tried his second long shot. It was, as a matter of fact, a good deal longer than the first, and when he put his question Ball thought he was asking something that was a virtual impossibility.

'You wouldn't still have anywhere a bullet or even a cartridge case that was fired from your Browning?'

He expected the other to shake his head. Instead, Rowland's face puckered in a frown, and he said, 'You know, I just might have at that.'

'How do you mean?' Ball asked.

'Well,' Rowland explained, 'I remember once going down to

the river just to fire some test shots. You know, try out the gun, how it felt and what sort of kick it had.'

Ball said nothing, though he couldn't see how shooting bullets into a river months before could conceivably help his case now.

Rowland went on slowly, like a man forcing his memory to yield something hard to recall. 'I brought home the spent cartridge cases, I remember, and some time later I found one in a drawer when I wanted to wind up some adhesive tape. You know, to make a core to wrap the tape round.'

'You mean you've still got it?' asked Ball, feeling his excitement growing.

'I don't know about got it,' John Rowland grinned. 'But it should be round the place somewhere, still with some of the tape wrapped round it.'

'You mean here?'

'No, in the house in Caernarvon.'

The upshot of this interview was that Superintendent John Ball was very soon journeying back to Wales. He went to Rowland's home and started to look in the likely places, and when this search surrendered nothing he wanted he began on the less likely places, and in one – a pocket of an old and discarded jacket – he came upon the cartridge case with several layers of adhesive tape wrapped round it.

It had been a long road, but he felt he had reached the end. It would be an incredible coincidence if the cartridge case revealed after the layers of adhesive tape had been peeled away did not match the one found on the carpet beside the dead woman in Chester Square.

When he arrived back in London with the cartridge case he felt there was a fair chance that, confronted with the facts, Boyce might forget to be stubborn and tell him where he had concealed the gun. If he could produce the gun and both cartridge cases no legal argument could break the case.

The two cartridge cases were tested in a comparison microscope in the police forensic laboratory. When the microscope was correctly adjusted it showed that the firing pin of the Browning had been slightly faulty in striking. It had made a peculiar mark that was identical on the bottom of each cartridge case.

In short, they matched as having been fired from the same gun.

Finding that tape-wrapped cartridge had been a piece of detective work that few writers of thrillers would have risked using in a fictitious crime. All Ball needed to round off his case was the gun.

But when he told the man being held pending further investigations all the gloomy Arthur Boyce would say was, 'I threw it in the sea to get rid of it.'

Well, as a painter engaged in decorating a seaside pier he certainly had plenty of opportunity. So no one could claim this was an unlikely act. Nor would the gun ever be recovered if Boyce had tossed the weapon into the sea from the end of the pier.

All that was left before the case could be brought to court was to supply a motive that made the whole thing appear a logical process towards violent death.

It has been claimed that Rawlings had about twenty plain-clothes men checking and investigating the background of this ill-starred pair of lovers. Already John Ball, in Boyce's Brighton lodgings, had sensed the man's irrational quality. This was supported by evidence that he had indulged himself in romantic illusions. He was married with a grown-up family and extremely slender resources. At the time he met and courted Elizabeth McLindon he had already served a sentence for bigamy, and had not long been released from prison. He bought her a number of expensive presents, yet his weekly wage as a painter in Brighton at that time was six pounds a week. He had a bank balance of seventy-five pounds, but he had altered the total to a more impressive £2,075.

He had made himself attentive and, strange as it may seem, attractive to Elizabeth McLindon, and she had agreed to marry this man who told her he was a bachelor. On 3 June, five days before her murder, she sent an announcement to her local paper in the North. It told of her forthcoming marriage to Arthur Robert Boyce. When she informed her sister in Liverpool the latter agreed to be the bridesmaid at the wedding ceremony. The woman who had passed forty made the first purchases for her trousseau.

That much was straightforward.

What was more involved was something else that happened on 3 June. A man rang up a West End jeweller and claimed to be speaking from the house of the Greek King, where he wanted some engagement rings to be delivered for consideration. One of the jeweller's assistants set off with a number of rings and was met at 45 Chester Square by a man who was later identified as the Brighton painter. He said he was the customer and chose a ring priced at £175 and made out a cheque for the purchase.

However, the assistant from the jeweller's shop became suspicious when the rather slovenly customer's pen fumbled when writing the word 'hundred' on the cheque, almost as though he was not sure of the spelling.

'We'll retain the ring until the cheque is cleared in the usual way,' the worldly-wise assistant said and departed with his complete collection of rings and the cheque with the smudged-looking word 'hundred' on it.

That cheque was not cleared, although it was presented twice. The first time its return was marked with the endorsement 'Figures illegible'. The second time, after initialling by Boyce, it just bounced with a large 'R.D.' stamped on it.

So it was referred to drawer by phone, but instead of Boyce, it was Elizabeth McLindon who took the call. That was on the fatal Saturday, 8 June.

The result of the mixed-up phone call could have been the removing of some rather thick scales from Elizabeth McLindon's eyes. Wherever she and Boyce ran to in the afternoon of that Saturday, they met later in the house that was to be visited by its royal tenant on the morrow. It is certain that Boyce arrived armed with the Browning because he knew the woman would never listen to his pleading, especially if she had found out about the bogus cheques and his former sentence for bigamy, and murder could be the only desperate way out of his dilemma.

There was a telephone at the dead woman's side when her body was found. It was considered at least possible that she was on the point of ringing the police when her murderer lifted his stolen weapon and killed her.

The stolen Browning was explained by Boyce at his Old Bailey trial as a weapon he had given Miss McLindon for her protection against those mysterious callers he had mentioned to

John Ball during their first meeting in Brighton. But to the man who had undertaken the investigation that had bared the truth about a callous killer the claims about mysterious callers and a possible assassin were merely part of that irrational romantic streak that ran through the prisoner's make-up. Arthur Boyce was a congenital liar, but his lies were all made to serve his inflated ego. Dropping the gun in the sea was forgotten.

He was a grubby little man who was worthless as a husband and useless as a father. He had wantonly involved a spinster nearing middle age in his false lure of romance and been dismayed by her complete aversion to his pitiless deceit when she had accidentally discovered the truth about him – as he had feared she would. For he had known she would receive any late telephone call from the jeweller's about the stumer cheque.

That had been the reason why he had haunted 45 Chester Square on the fatal Saturday. He couldn't avoid disaster. Nor could Elizabeth McLindon.

Derek Curtis-Bennett, KC, did his best for Boyce when he strove to interest the jury in a reasonable doubt based on a stranger shooting the dead woman with the weapon Boyce had given her for her protection.

This was a development of the mysterious callers theory that Boyce had started in his lodging in Brighton. His counsel couldn't make it sound convincing, however, for too much depended on supposition and there was no supposition in the case John Ball and the other Yard men had made out. At least, that was what the jury felt when after considering the evidence they returned to announce their verdict.

' Guilty.'

No one was really surprised. The fanciful alternative suggested by the prisoner's counsel had not made any real impact on anyone who heard it, except perhaps the stunned prisoner, for whom fancy was a way of life from which he had proved himself unable to change, inside prison or out.

Arthur Robert Boyce rose in the dock and stood loose-limbed and trembling to hear the judge sentence him to pay the only price the law demanded at that time. Three weeks later he was hanged.

Rawlings continued his career at the Yard and eventually

followed Hugh Young as the Commander in charge of the Yard's CID when Prothero's assistant in the Southampton garage murder retired. The former PC 541 had reached the topmost rung of the police promotional ladder. Heading the Yard team that solved Miss McLindon's murder had not caused his climbing steps to stumble.